For the African craftsmen
whose lives have become a part of our own

Also by Esther Warner Dendel

The Basic Book of Fingerweaving
Needleweaving, Easy as Embroidery
The Crossing Fee: *A Story of Liberia*
Art: An Everyday Experience
The Silk-Cotton Tree (*a novel*)
Seven Days to Lomaland: *Personal Experience in West Africa*
New Song in a Strange Land: *Discovering Hinterland Culture in Liberia*

For Margaret
with love,
Esther
"
Esther Warner
Dendel
Nov. 1975.

African Fabric Crafts

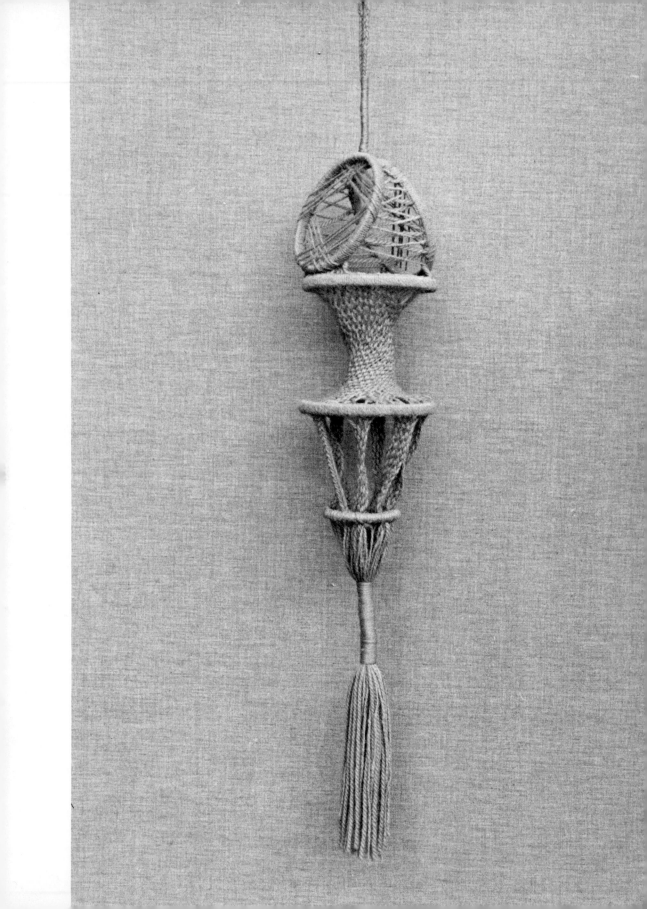

African Fabric Crafts

SOURCES OF AFRICAN DESIGN AND TECHNIQUE

Esther Warner Dendel

with drawings and photographs by Jo Dendel

Taplinger Publishing Company / New York

Photographic Credits

The author is grateful to these museums, institutions, and
photographers for permission to reproduce illustrations not available
in Jo Dendel's collection:

Courtesy of *African Arts,* photograph by John Goldblatt: page 45, and
    color facing page 64
Courtesy of The Brooklyn Museum: page 80
Courtesy of the Field Museum of Natural History, Chicago: pages 140
    and 152
Courtesy of the Museum of Cultural History, UCLA; photograph by
    Larry Dupont: page 42
Courtesy of the Milwaukee Public Museum: page 154
Courtesy of the Museum of the Philadelphia Civic Center: page 150
Courtesy of the Museum of Primitive Art, New York; photograph by
    Charles Uht: page 27
Photographs by Rick Davis: pages 22 and 93.

First Edition

Published in the United States in 1974 by
TAPLINGER PUBLISHING CO., INC.
New York, New York

Published simultaneously in the Dominion of Canada by
Burns & MacEachern, Ltd., Toronto

Library of Congress Catalog Card Number: 72-6627

ISBN 0-8008-0150-4

Lithographed by The Murray Printing Company, Forge Village, Massachusetts

Designed by Mollie M. Torras

Contents

Illustrations in Color

Foreword

I would like to tell you about a few moments of African learning. The scene was by a stream in Liberia. I was sitting on the sandy bank enjoying the early morning sunlight and the activity all about me. Rain had fallen during the night. I awoke to the sound of rivulets smoothing down the thatch roof above my head. Now it was morning and every leaf was shining, washed clean.

The women of the village had brought their laundry to the stream. Water purled over the rocks where the women stood, naked and bright in the sun. They were splashed with silver droplets each time they slapped their garments smartly against the flat stones.

Sitting all around me on the sand were naked children, strangely subdued after having exhausted themselves with water-play. They were playing a different game now with quiet intensity. Each child had a little stick in his hand with which he was drawing a braid pattern in the sand. The entire design had to be made without lifting the stick; this was the rule of the game. The other rule was that there be no beginning or end to the design when it was finished; beginning and end must become part of the same line.

Beside me, keenly watching each child in turn, was the old man I had learned to call Pa during our travels together over the forest trails. This was his home village to which we had come at last after many days of walking. He was Pa to all of them as he was to me.

While the women laughed and sang and splashed and pounded, the old man's glance darted from child to child. When a stick wobbled uncertainly, when a line lost its symmetry, when the end did not join with the beginning, he appeared to wince as though some aching nerve deep in his body had twitched. He did not rise to help with a single problem but his eyes looked encouragement. And when lines that were meant to meet did not, there was a drawn, pained look on his face as though he felt some old wound.

I sensed that these little trails in the sand had some cosmic significance. Did they symbolize wholeness? Balance? Life without end? I did not dare intrude upon his concentration by asking.

When the women had finished their work and hung their lengths of cloth on the bushes to dry, they started back to the village. The children left with them but not until every pattern in the sand had been patted back to smoothness. The old man motioned that I was to stay beside him. He picked up one of the sticks and traced out with great delicacy of motion a perfect pattern of the kind the children had attempted.

"So," he said, "in this way we would have our life. Babies are born. They travel the path of their days. They die. They come to us again in the new babies born. With luck, the path is even. With luck, there is no break."

"But if there are stones on the path, Pa? What then? Does the path turn to go around the stones?"

He smoothed out the sand and made a new design with his stick. It was quite different from the first. Some lines started and went forward in a wobbly way and turned back toward the beginning. Other lines came together in a tangle as though a knot had been tied. There were lines that hesitated and lines that trailed off into nothing. With a gesture of impatience, the old man scuffed the whole pattern out with his foot.

"This is the way of life when people do not give ear to the ways of the old ones. These are bad times. People quarrel and make knots. People fear and turn back. The end and the beginning do not come to-

Beaded garments that belonged to the late Oba, Abimbolu Afolade II, of Ode Remo in Ijebu Province, Western State, Nigeria

gether in the proper way." He threw his stick in the stream and we started back to the village.

I had received a fine lesson in symbolism as well as the activity of lines to which meanings were attached. I had seen the African way of teaching and of learning at work.

Years later I stood in the foyer of the National Museum in Lagos. Before me was a magnificent beaded costume that had belonged to a late Oba (chief) in Ijebu province. A beaded crown was surmounted by sixteen beaded birds in the traditional style. The caftan was a typical Yoruba garment. Many square feet of fabric were used. Embroidered on it were over a million little beads. The designs were those I had first seen drawn in the sand at the waterside in Liberia. The embroidery simulated the "overs and unders" of a braid, the involvement of strands without beginning or end. My old Pa would have called it proper.

To this day, I cannot cross one fiber over another or involve one set of threads with another without remembering the host of proverbs that apply. One strand lies on top of another. I see this but what I hear with memory's ear is, "Our elders are on top of [above] us." Or, "No matter how long the night, the day will come to the top [surface as in the meandering strands of a braid]." Or, "He who learns, teaches."

This African passion for imbuing the smallest act with significance seems to be a beautiful way to live. Their meanings are not our meanings; we must find our own, each of us. It is the search for meanings in

Detail of braid design worked in beads

what we do that ties the craftsmen of all cultures into a world fellowship.

One further concept, the most important of all, I think, is the African talent for sensing *mana,* or spirit, in all materials, as well as in themselves. *Mana* is a word that anthropologists use when they want to talk about a certain quality they have observed in African and other preindustrial societies. The dictionary defines it as "an impersonal supernatural force inherent in gods and sacred objects."

Among African craftsmen, the meaning of *mana* is both wider and deeper than this definition. The human and the spiritual (as we tend to think of the meanings of those words) are intermingled; in fact they are scarcely distinguished. All acts, even the way one stirs a cooking pot, are spiritual acts with deep meanings. Spiritual force flows from the doer to the material. But just as important, there is a countercurrent from the material to the hand of the worker, the craftsman, the cook, the woman weeding her rice farm. A woman with evil thoughts can spoil the food she is cooking because badness passes from her arm through the stirring spoon into the food. In the same way, a cooking pot that was not formed in joy and with love for the clay will emanate a sourness capable of spoiling the food as well as the mind of the cook.

Two pots made by two different women may look identical, yet one is a good pot and one is not. What makes the difference and the destiny of each pot is the quality of spirit in the potter. In Liberia, a desirable pot is made by a woman who goes in the early morning in a spirit of humility to the swamp where the clay "lives." The woman goes without clothing to demonstrate her humility before sacred earth. She must beg the clay to forgive her for disturbing it and taking it to a new place. She will explain her people's need for new pots and explain that they are prepared to take good care of them. She will promise the clay that none of it will be wasted and that after it becomes a pot, it will be washed every day and that after its bath it will be set in the sun to sweeten.

After the clay is scooped up and carried to the village, it will not be coiled until the woman is at ease within herself because an agitated spirit will cause a pot to crack in the fire. The African concept of *mana* is operating continuously from the time the clay is taken from the swamp until it has ceased to hold food for the woman's family.

The African way of seeing spirit in all things is perhaps possible to craftsmen even in our overindustrialized society. It places an emphasis on feeling one's energy directed toward and flowing into material.

Forming material and shaping it with one's hands is a giving out and a taking in. More than that, it is a spiritualizing of one's energy through rhythmic motion. This is, above all, what we have tried to feel in using African techniques in our own way.

The we I speak of is a group with which I have worked closely for many years. It revolves around our own studio and we call ourselves the Denwar Craft Fellowship. A number of this group have traveled to Africa with me to meet craftsmen across the continent. The bulk of the work produced for this book came from this reaching out of hands, hands that want to touch other hands, hands that want to know the feel of materials, hands that form and make, hands that exert and receive energy from the process.

Some of the African craftsmen are anonymous, men and women we know only through their work. Some of that work came to us through the privilege of seeing the great collection put together by the Museum of Modern Art for its 1972–1973 show African Textiles and Decorative Arts. Many of the Africans whose work has excited us are artists who shared their skills with me during the years I lived in Liberia. Some are new friends met during return trips to Liberia and other parts of Africa. Contemporary African art is an exciting scene and it is a joy to see young craftsmen reaching out for new ways of expression.

1

Appliqué ~
The Art of Assembling Scraps

A certain humility is attached to the fabric arts of Africa, even when cloth is assembled into the sumptuous robes of chiefs and royalty. African fibers are the bounty of the Earth Mother—cotton, raffia, bark, wool from goats, camels, and sheep. Their silk is wild, collected in the bush. They are honest stuffs and that honesty is part of their great appeal.

A great deal of feeling, *mana* if you will, goes into each of the hand processes necessary to produce African cloth. Many years ago when I lived in Africa, I visited a remote village in Liberia where thirty of the chief's wives were sitting on mats in his compound, carding cotton. Each woman had a hunting bow. By placing the cotton on the bow string and flipping it, the dense little wads of cotton, from which the seeds had been rolled out, were fluffed into airy lightness. Piles of carded cotton appeared on every mat looking like fallen puffs of cloud. Three women were sitting together at one side, doing nothing. They looked deprived and desolate in contrast to the happy expressions on the faces of the working women. I asked the chief about them.

"Today, they have stones in their hearts," he said. This is a country saying that is used to describe what we call depression. "If those women touch the cotton it will also become like little stones—hard. A woman has to be big with glad before she can make the cotton swell big."

"How can a woman throw stones out of her heart?" I asked this, wondering whether in any culture there was a known cure for the malaise.

"It is not a thing a woman can do for herself," the old chief said. "All of us must help. Tonight the drums will talk. They will lift the feet. If a woman refuses to have her feet lifted, the drums will do it anyway, whether the woman agrees or not. The drums pound. The feet of the women pound the ground. The men will beat the ground with sticks and the women will dance. The pounding will throw the stones out of hearts where any stones lie. Tomorrow I will allow those women to work."

I wished that I might have stayed that night in the village to hear the earth pounded, to listen, and to imagine that little hard pellets of sadness were splattering the packed earth of the compound like hail.

After women finish carding the cotton crop, they spin it into thread. Again, only happy women may pick up their spindles. A woman with bad thoughts, jealous thoughts, unhappiness, will cause the thread to snarl and twist back on itself.

When the women have finished spinning, the men take the thread and weave it into narrow strips. These are sewed, edge to edge, to make the lovely fabric which in Liberia is called country cloth. On our return trips over the years, I find less and less country cloth made of hand-spun thread. Most of it now is made from imported, machine-spun thread. I count each cloth I was able to collect in the 1940s a treasure beyond price. Some of the joyousness of women who were not allowed to touch the cotton unless they were happy seems to have stayed in the fibers.

Even when they handle imported cloth, African craftsmen seem to have a sure instinct, an ear for "what the cloth says." Not only yardage, but tiny scraps can be made to "talk." What these scraps say in the appliqués of Dahomey is the history of a people—a delightful and pain-less way to learn one's history.

In Dahomey, certain men of the Fon people of Abomey were the

*A large Dahomey banner
from the collection of Dr. Joanne Eicher*

makers of appliqué. Abomey was the ancient capital city of the kingdom. The stitchers lived in compounds near the palace of the kings. They made hangings, banners, caps, umbrellas, and ritual clothing.

The king who first extended his kingdom to the sea was Agadja, who ruled from 1708 to 1740. He was the first to deal with Europeans, so a sailing ship became his insignia. Other kings are represented as totem animals. Akaba, the last king to rule before the Europeans came, is represented in the hangings as a boar. His father is shown as a fish near a trap. Proverbs and sayings were invented to put meaning into the emblems of each king. One saying that goes with the fish beside the wicker trap is "The fish who escapes the trap does not return." It is the duty of every Fon father to instruct his sons in the sayings and the symbolism of the history banners.

The old kingdoms are broken and gone. The stitchers still stitch, their needles held between thumb and finger and pulled away from the body.

A running stitch, a back stitch, or a chain stitch is used. The customers now are not kings, but mainly tourists. The quality of the workmanship seems less good. At least we found no banners in 1973 which had the quality of the one collected by Dr. Joanne Eicher. But the idea of history in banner form excites us. It might well be a family history or a personal history. There are endless possibilities. Schools, families, and individuals can find in this project a way to pour meanings into scraps of cloth. I hope to do a banner of this sort for the children of our own family. It will have a white house, a big red barn, lots of chickens, pigs, and cows, a one-room schoolhouse, a sled, a Model T Ford, a tool house. The wood curls from my father's plane may well have been the reason I am a craftsman today. Farms are not like this in Iowa now and it is good to think back upon those things that helped to form one.

In the town of Oshogbo in Nigeria a sizable group of young men are working in a contemporary manner as individual craftsmen in many media. Among them is Samuel Ojo. He uses a sewing machine instead of a thumb-held needle. His subjects are derived from Yoruba folklore and myths and are filtered through his lively imagination. In his

Appliqué of drummers by Samuel Ojo from the collection of Betty Schumacher

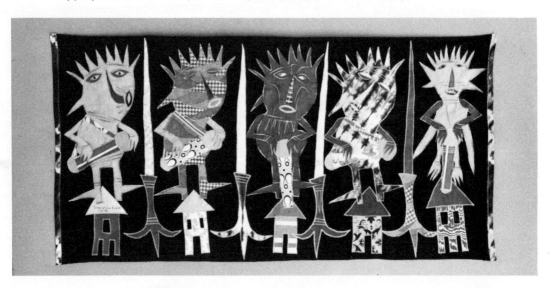

*Detail of Samuel Ojo appliqué showing
the use of a print in the eyes*

hangings we see recognizable houses and musical instruments, but his musicians are not of this world. He mixes plain and patterned commercial fabrics with odds and ends of tie-dye and batik against a unifying dark background. In the hanging shown we sense the glee of the little houses which seem to be doing their sturdy best to join the dance, a feat the drummers have already accomplished in defiance of all the rules of gravity.

Happenings in printed fabrics suggest to Ojo other things they may become. A white pattern in a curve suggests eyes. Never mind that in the original these may have been the petals of a flower.

In our summer workshop after the first African trip with our American craftsmen, we decided to try an experiment with fabric scraps. Everyone was asked to bring whatever small pieces he had. We were to look at each scrap in a new way—as a shape in its own right. The only rule for the game was that except for cutting holes in it, the shape was not to be changed. We found that even turning under the edges changed what was seen at first glance. The objective was to spark imaginative seeing. The product did not concern us as much as the process.

Lacking in our culture the rich heritage of mythology that the

A banner from negative or not-cut-on-purpose scraps by Tanya Baker

Yorubas have, it is a further exercise in imagination to make up stories and tales about the figures which emerge. Children are very good at this kind of play and through it adults can recover some of the spontaneity of childhood. The secret is to think of it as play, not as art.

We found that when we tried to cut shapes from yardage instead of using what happened to be left over, the shapes were less inspiring. After her first banner Tanya Baker made a blouse with appliqué shapes that she cut "on purpose." The garment is handsome but she felt even more excitement in seeing what she could do with the leftover scraps. And from them she composed a banner of African animals, fish, and birds. Alpha Salveson went to the Goodwill to forage for scraps. She

*Tanya Baker, who had met Samuel Ojo,
came up with a banner which is a first cousin
to his work yet completely her own.
The stitchery of machine sewing with orange
thread unites the diverse forms with one another
and with the background.*

"Transformation" by Alpha Salveson

Photograph by Rick Davis

found what she wanted in assorted blues, gray blues, and emerald green. Someone had cut what appeared to be a pair of slacks, abandoned before they were sewed. The only cutting Alpha did in the material she found was to shorten the leg of one of the pant sections. By combining these pieces in an ingenious way and doing a little stitchery to hold the composition together, she achieved a hanging, "Transformation," which has won many awards.

Without intending it and without knowing how it might turn out, Ellen Tanney's appliqué turned into a mythological hunter. This figure illustrates as exactly as though she had been working toward it a Liberian tale about a great hunter who accomplished supernatural feats when he went to the bush to hunt game.

He had only one eye, which was located in the middle of his head. His ears were pointed, which enabled him to hear the daintiest footfall of an antelope at incredible distances. People thought that having only one eye must surely be a handicap and they gave the credit for his prowess to his unusual ears. His real magic, however, centered in his stomach, which he kept covered with a robe except when he hunted. No one in his village knew that there were two more eyes and a mouth in his stomach.

An accidental, mythological hunter by Ellen Tanney

When I go again to Liberia, I hope to carry this appliqué to tell people there how their Great Hunter accidentally became part of our life. The only thing they will question is that it happened accidentally.

For those of us who sew it takes an effort and a new way of looking at fabrics before we can enjoy raveling much less revel in raveling. In defense of raw edges, it is certainly apparent that the warp and the weft, which are tightly involved with one another in the weaving process, when raveled and separated have a chance to show their own identity. This is often a surprise one does not anticipate, especially if the warp is a different color and texture than the weft. I have come, at last, to the conclusion that no fabric can be truly appreciated unless one does ravel some edges.

A glorious example of letting scraps, raveled at the edges, speak for themselves is a composition in cloth by the artist Jan Peters. It is laden with personal symbolism and was done especially for Laura De Lacy. The garment on which the scraps were applied was a hand-loomed *huipil* from Mexico. It is a coarse cotton with wonderful undulating wefts in parts of the weaving. The bright colors of the appliqué repeat the colors of the hand embroidery that was on the sleeves when the garment was purchased. A delightful concession to warm weather and body movement was made by leaving the sleeves unsewn in the arm-hole area.

Appliqué on a Mexican huipil by Jan Peters for Laura De Lacy

Another appliqué was also done on a Mexican garment, a full-sleeved shirt. Julia George's forte is batik and tie-dye. The design in a batik which she did not consider successful in itself suggested areas to cut away. Some of these cutout shapes were replaced before the entire composition was sewn down with machine stitching.

Tie-dye scraps machine-appliquéd on a shirt by Julia George

This detail shows the free use of a galloping sewing machine.

Although appliqué is made and enjoyed all over the world and certainly is not exclusively African, we do have, because of our African experience, two unique ways to use the technique and a fresh excitement about it. The first is the idea of making history banners inspired by those of Dahomey. The second is a new way of looking at scraps. This has been sparked by the joyful creations of Samuel Ojo of Oshogbo.

Appliqué with scraps has much to recommend it. All ages can enjoy it. It costs almost nothing. It promotes playful activity both in individuals and in groups. It is a joyous thing to do. In our culture we do not pound the earth to toss stones of sadness out of our hearts but we may be able to "grow big with glad," like the wives in the chief's compound, if we are willing to give ourselves to the cloth and let it do the talking.

2

When Less Is More –
Subtractive Embroidery

Cutting holes in fabric or pulling out threads may seem at first thought a strange way to make fabric more beautiful. How can less add up to more? A thoughtful study of this Hausa robe reveals that much has been taken away and much has been added to make an incredibly beautiful and rich surface. The embroidered section of the robe is 40 inches wide. The large cut circles and the numerous small holes, which are apparently punched in the fabric, are encircled and entwined by innumerable small lines of directional stitching, which gives the effect of quilting.

Subtractive embroidery done in a manner which completely changes the character of the surface of the fabric is perhaps one of the finest examples of the African concept of *mana* at work, of effort and response between craftsman and material. It is a basic language both visual and visceral which is possible in all the arts, but particularly in the fabric arts.

The same kind of transformation was used in the making of a vest from a loosely woven material. Some of the fabric was cut and raveled

26

Hausa robe. Courtesy of the Museum of Primitive Art in New York

*Vest of subtractive embroidery made by
Cindy Seefeld under the direction of her instructor,
Jean Stange, at the right, a detail of the vest*

vertically and some horizontally. Wrapping the released fibers contributed to the textural quality.

Unbleached muslin was used to make a blouse with a more limited amount of stitchery. Circles were cut out of the material after the blouse was cut. The edges of the detached circles of fabric were turned

*Unbleached muslin blouse by
Sharon Berg*

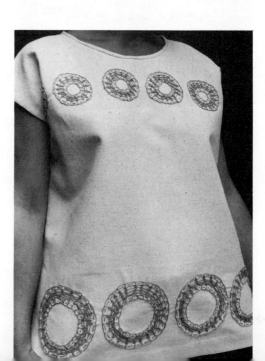

under and basted, as were the edges of the circle from which they were cut out. Linen thread in natural color was used and the bastings remain part of the decoration. Looping was used to rejoin the circles to the areas from which they had been cut. In the Hausa robe, crocheting appears to be the rejoining technique. Blanket stitching is another possibility.

After studying the Hausa robe Helen Trescott did a wall hanging in white thread worked over and into off-white fabric. Some of the circles had their cutout centers replaced and some did not. The completed embroidery was mounted over a thin plywood board. The fabric showing through the cutout areas is a blue and green tie-dye fabric in subtle shadings. She found that the work was more manageable when she pinned the separate sections to a piece of white paper which kept all the spacings under control during the reassembling.

White on white hanging

Another variation of the Hausa technique was done by cutting many small holes in the yoke of a dress and finishing the edges with close-set blanket stitch. Feather stitching meanders between and connects the separate circles.

Variation of the Hausa technique in a dress yoke by Bici Linklater

Virginia Thorne of Illinois gives workshops in a technique she calls "needle lace in space." She begins by cutting a round hole in a square of stiff, smooth cardboard. A circle about 7 inches in diameter is cut in the center of a 12-inch-square cardboard with a razor blade or other sharp cutter. A piece of coarse woven fabric, hop sacking or heavy linen, is cut slightly larger than the cardboard so that the edges may be bent back over the cardboard. A hole just slightly smaller than the one cut in the cardboard is cut into the cloth. Sometimes buttonhole stitches

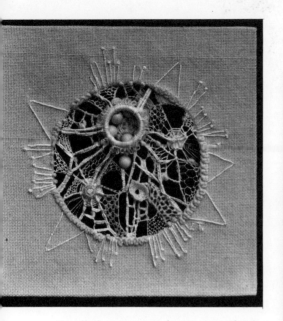

Needle lace in space by Virginia Thorne

The detailed photograph shows how plain, unknotted looping has been combined with the "knitted look" looping that is knotted, and looping that is twisted.

are made around the circle before the center is cut out. Or, a row of sewing machine stitchery may be used to firm up the edge.

Needle weaving, embroidery, bone curtain rings, and white buttons may all be used in the area or space where the cloth is cut away. Looping in several varieties of this technique is a common way to reweave the space. She places emphasis on having a good variety of textures in threads before beginning work—thick thread, thin thread, shiny, dull, smooth, and fuzzy, all in the same color.

Bula Rollyson started her subtractive embroidery after studying the Hausa robe, but the result is quite different in effect. Warp threads which were snipped and raveled back in the white woolen material were rewoven with a brown yarn. Quite by accident, these reconstructed areas began to resemble arms and legs and the parka-rimmed head of an Eskimo. Threads were pulled at the top of the hanging to reveal the color and texture of the weathered wood used as a hanger. Some pulling of threads and weaving back with brown yarn made use of the areas of background fabric on either side of the figure.

"Eskimo" by Bula Rollyson

Charla Rudolph added padded areas which were appliquéd to the surface of her wall hanging in subtractive embroidery. Additional texture was achieved by attaching bleached bones from a chicken neck at strategic points of the design.

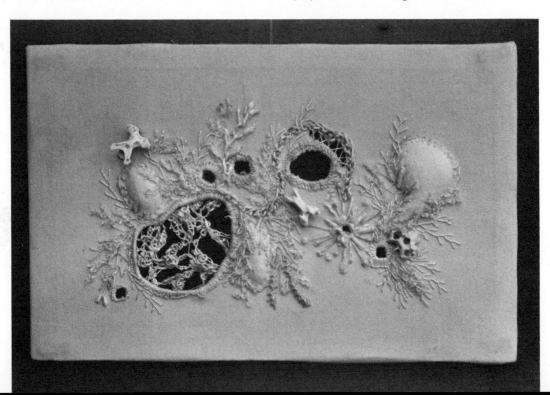

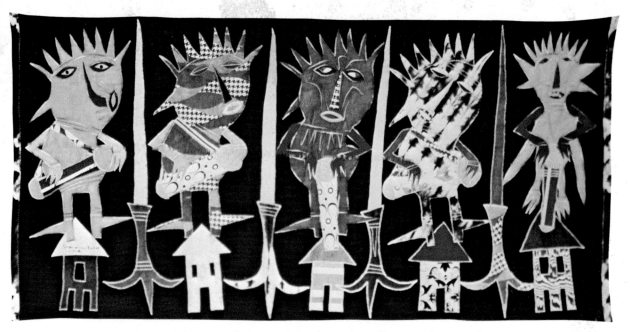

Appliqué of drummers by Samuel Ojo from the collection of Betty Schumacher

Detail of accidental appliqué from negative shapes by Tanya Baker

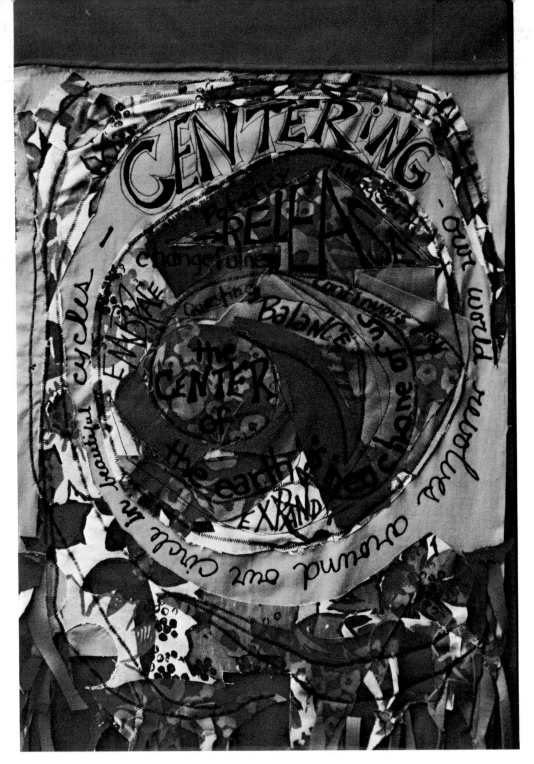

Collage of tie-dye scraps and machine stitching by Julia George.
Words are reminders of a meaningful book.

One of the most interesting pieces of subtractive work in fabric has no embroidery at all. It is from Dr. Joanne Eicher's collection and was acquired by her on the island of Buguma when she lived in Nigeria. The original fabric was a woven pattern of dark squares separated by white lines. By selective snipping and pulling of threads an entirely new design was made.

Pattern of African cloth formed by pulling threads, from the collection of Dr. Joanne Eicher. The detail shows how both vertical and horizontal threads were eliminated.

3

Adinkira ~ Saying It with Symbols

Adinkira is a patterned fabric made by stamping designs on the surface of cloth. It is an Asanti (formerly Ashanti) craft and is used to make magnificent wraparound costumes which are worn like Roman togas.

Sometimes bands of cloth 14 inches wide (after the edges are folded under in a double hem) are fastened together with a fagoting stitch in bright colors of thread. This is done before the stamping and automatically makes spatial divisions running the length of the cloth. The long strips are further divided by parallel lines which are made with the teeth of a carved wooden comb, dipped in dye. The dye is made from the bark of a tree boiled in water until it is thick as tar. The stamps are carved from small sections of calabash. Repeat patterns are sometimes made of crossed lines formed by dragging the comb first

A section of adinkira cloth with a band of fagoting, parallel lines, the comb used to make the lines, and four of the carved calabash stamps

in one direction and then in the other so the lines intersect at right angles.

Almost fifty years ago when Robert Rattray wrote his *Religion and Art in Ashanti*, fifty-three separate *adinkira* designs were shown in his book and the meanings behind them were explained. In 1973 when our craftsmen went to visit the village outside Kumasi where *adinkira* stamping is a specialty, we found many of the same designs in use which Robert Rattray had described. No one really knows how long these same symbols have been used.

One of the legends about the making and wearing of *adinkira* is that there was a ruler, King Adinkira, who ruled Guyaman, which is now part of the Ivory coast. There was a battle around the beginning of the nineteenth century in which King Adinkira was killed. Presumably the Asantis took his robe for a trophy and named the cloth after him. For many years *adinkira* cloth was associated with mourning. The word *dinkra* means good-bye. Wearing the cloth was a way to give farewell to the deceased. The cloth is now worn at any time and not restricted to periods of grief.

Perhaps the most interesting use of the cloth was to show an attitude or a mood. The fern pattern was associated with the saying, "I am independent of you." By wearing a cloth patterned with the fern motif, a man was indicating to all who saw him how he felt about himself and others on that particular day.

It is an exciting experience to visit an *adinkira* village. Piles of bark lie about ready to be boiled to make the dye. A battery of gasoline cans are lined up on parallel rows of mud curbing. A plume of smoke rises from the burning logs under the cans. Here the bark is boiled in water throughout the day.

Stretched taut between two trees were two lengths of fabric being embroidered together. The tension keeps the edges of the sections curled tightly under. One of the most lasting impressions from a day in the village is the memory of how rhythmically everything is done. The flash of the hand holding the stamp as it moves from the dye to the cloth and back to the dye is something one does not forget. Like almost everything that is done expertly, this looks easy. It becomes a clumsy motion only when one tries to do it oneself.

Most subtle of all the *adinkira* patterns is a flowerlike shape of four petals done on black fabric without any embroidery. Four of these simple shapes stamped in a square give the illusion of a center motif.

The stitcher's fingers flew so fast we had to ask him to slow down so we could see exactly how the stitch was made.

Intersecting lines made with a wooden comb dipped in dye

Each stamp is a complete design, a unit in itself. By clustering the repeats of each unit, various textures are achieved.

Patterning by stamping is an old art and not exclusively African by any means. What impressed us about *adinkira* stamping, in addition to the expertness of the craftsmen and the ingenious way in which they use what is available, is the symbolism attached to the motifs.

In our own culture we can experience stamping techniques with materials available to us. Calabashes may not be easily found. An excellent substitute is made by cutting shapes from sponge cloth. This is a synthetic sponge in flat sheets which is sold with cleaning supplies. The cloth may be cut with ordinary scissors and is easy to manage. One of our group cut her own symbols from sponge cloth and glued them onto her children's blocks. She used acrylic paint to do her stamping. Another used an automobile gasket to make a set of symbols for her stamping. Some of the motifs were borrowed from African textiles, others were of her own invention.

Symbols cut from sponge cloth and glued to children's blocks by Ellen Tanney

Hanging stamped with bicycle parts in blue and green acrylic

An owl combining stamping and machine stitchery on tie-dye by Julia George

Found objects may be used in imaginative ways. Fran Curl found bicycle parts which she made into stamps by varnishing them and then powdering flocking material over them while the varnish was still wet. The wet varnish acted as an adhesive.

Either oil-base printing ink or acrylic paint may be used. If printing ink is used the extender made by the manufacturer should be used for

Irma Switzer used the stamps she had purchased in Ghana to make an adinkira bedspread. The fabric is muslin and the pigment oil-base printing ink.

The Northern knot is the third pattern down from the neck in the center of the garment.

thinning it rather than adding turpentine. Sometimes the pigment is painted on with a brush. Sometimes the paint is applied to a pad of fabric and the stamp is pressed against this inked pad.

A number of *adinkira* symbols collected by Irma Switzer in Ghana were used to decorate a blouse. One of the symbols, sometimes called the Northern knot, is seen in many media in West Africa. It is sometimes used to pattern the concrete railings on porches in Nigeria. We have been given various meanings for the symbol. Usually it is said to imply unity or interdependence.

A study of the designs used in *adinkira* stamping gives one a good vocabulary of shapes which may be used for other purposes. Learning to think symbolically is a way to enrich thought and to add depth to personal experience. It has been said that symbols are not invented but discovered. What *adinkira* cloth has to teach us about the use of symbolism in ordinary life is even more important than the stamping technique itself. Symbolic discoveries are the business of the poet. As we master something of his art, we bring poetry and song into the bleak and mundane.

4

Magic in Words and in Ink

In a gallery in Ghana we saw a warrior's shirt made long ago of hand-loomed cotton fabric. It had become tobacco color from age and use. The surface bristled with small packets which contained writing. We were told that these written words, most of which were verses from the Koran, had great power—power enough to turn aside arrows aimed at the wearer, power enough to blunt bullets.

The magic in words had brought the wearer through many dusty battles, including a skirmish with the British and their gleaming weaponry. I asked our informant whether the word packets would protect anyone who owned the jacket. Would they protect or have an influence on me, for instance, if I bought the jacket. His answer was very serious. "No, mama. You have got to believe the words. I think you live by different words."

The Museum of Cultural History at UCLA owns a warrior jacket and hat much like those we have seen in Ghana. Another garment which combines leather amulets and written script was collected in

Warrior's jacket much like the one we had seen in Ghana. Courtesy of the Museum of Cultural History, UCLA

1889 and comes from Senegal. It was included in the Museum of Modern Art's show of African Textiles and Decorative Arts.

These garments made a deep impression on those of us who saw them. During our summer workshop after our first African trip we asked ourselves some questions about words, about the part they play in shaping what we do and feel. By what words do we live? This question is intensely personal and the answer varies from person to person. I know that certain words and certain poems have a living meaning to me and that there is a magic in them which does protect against life's difficulties and which does blunt assaults which are not as dramatic as British weaponry, but wounding nevertheless.

In writing about his childhood, Camera Laye, the author of *Dark Child*, describes how his father, a goldsmith, went about making an ornament. The father had skill of hand, but for all his skill the ornament was without value until the proper words had been said over it. Spoken words turned a thing into something more than an object. Life force entered the metal with the incantation. The word was imperative.

In our own society words have been cheapened by overuse. We

seem to talk more and to say less. Contrasting this spill of words with the veneration felt for words in African cultures, it seemed to us a worthy thing to collect and store words which vibrate with meaning.

Some words have utility, but no magic. Some which had magic during other periods of one's life may have lost their luster. Many of the words one lives by are in a continual state of flux as the mind gropes and grows. Banners, which by their very nature and materials are rather temporary, seemed one way to capture thoughts of growth and transformation.

One of our group, Julia George, discovered a book that spoke to her with clarity and beauty. The author of *Centering*, Mary Caroline Richards, is both a potter and a poet. Her images come from the potter's craft but speak to all craftsmen, regardless of medium. This book inspired a collage banner from tie-dye and batik scraps on which Julia wrote words and snatches of thought which recall entire paragraphs and sentences from *Centering*. Black Inkodye was used for the lettering on the bright scraps, which are held in place with lines of sewing machine stitchery.

Collage banner by Julia George

 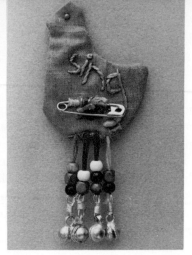

The thought behind the pin is a secret between the pin and the wearer.

A fabric bird pin by Karen Raines

Ink has long been a venerated substance in Africa, partly because it is used in Koranic schools to write sacred verses on wooden slates. Usually, the verses are in Arabic, which the teacher neither reads nor understands, but the words are held in such high regard that the water used to wash the ink from the slates is collected in containers and used for medicine.

Words on fabric after the pattern was cut and before sewing, by Judy Whelan

"Yemosa: Mother of Reproduction"
by Twins Seven Seven

Photograph by John Goldblatt,
reprinted from *African Arts,*
Vol. VI, No. 1

Although the young, contemporary African artists may not assign mystic qualities to ink, it is a natural medium to which they turn. Twins Seven Seven, the best known of the group of artists to come from the Nigerian town of Oshogbo, began his first work in ink and it remains his favorite material. Professor Ulli Beier explains in his book, *Contemporary Art in Africa,* that while everyone else involved in their art workshop was making swooping sloshes with large brushes, Twins Seven Seven was drawing thin black lines with a little twig he had found. He was quickly given pen and ink. His first picture shows the same kind of inspired doodling which characterizes his work today.

When our group of craftsmen visited Twins's home and studio in 1973, he said that what he would like to share with us was his entire life style, not just his painting. He is a spectacular dancer, he composes music, leads his own band, designs his own clothing, and makes up long stories to explain the fantastic creatures he draws. Twins's imagination seems without limit. Visiting him opens up a new vista of art as process, as a way of life. This concept may be the greatest of all of Africa's great contributions to creative thinking.

Z. K. Oloruntoba, whose style resembles that of Twins, does work that stands on its own, strong in design and delightful in its allusions. The one in our collection has a fragment of a Yoruba story pinned to the back. It relates that when a women hunter chanced to come upon some antelopes in the forest, they were busy changing themselves into dancing ghosts. Teeth are an important design motif in Z. K. Oloruntoba's works. Indeed, teeth figure prominently in many Yoruba stories.

Ink on fabric by Z. K. Oloruntoba

A woman may change into nothing but a huge set of teeth strong enough to cut down trees. Nigerian folk tales tell of many kinds of transformations. Demon lovers in animal shapes turn into handsome young men. Palm trees dance. It is a wondrous world where anything is possible. The daydream spirit of doodling makes it a suitable way to illustrate a fairyland which is also very real.

Twins Seven Seven draws his themes largely from these ancient Yoruba legends and from his own heightened versions of the old tales. Anything that passes through his head seems to come out in a brighter, livelier form. Inspired by his work and by conversation with him, our group undertook an experiment in doodling. Almost all of us doodle but we do it without any purpose or intent. Our attitude has been that a doodle isn't supposed to mean anything or be anything, certainly not art. Thus, many people who would hesitate to begin anything called a drawing will doodle. A doodle is approached in a playful way and this makes it a good path to experimentation in design.

Studying our own attempts at doodling heightened our appreciation for the ones we had seen in Africa. Most of us tended to repeat little shapes all of which were about the same size with lines that were about the same width. We did not in the beginning have a vocabulary of shapes or motifs. Nothing we did could compare in interest to Twins Seven Seven's first drawing. We decided that we needed to accumulate ideas for patterning since they did not seem to spring from our pens spontaneously.

An enormous amount of inspiration for design exists not only in the traditional patterned fabrics of Africa but in almost everything Africans make. Spoons, carved calabashes, gold weights, pendants, the designs incised in pottery, relief designs on mud walls, even a small detail of a carved house post or mask abounds in idea-making detail.

After a study of African motifs, Jean Hudson utilized a number of them in a caftan she made of white nylon lining. The voluminous quality of the garment of 7 yards of 45-inch-wide material is in keeping with the African idea of creativity. Among the Yoruba of Nigeria, the god Obtala, whose essence is endless creativity, is symbolized by a white cloth so large it is impossible to fold it.

The fabric she used was so sheer a design on paper could be seen through the cloth. This eliminated the need to trace the motifs directly on the material. Each side is a mirror image of the other. The motifs include the famous Bambara antelope heads, turtles, lizards, snakes,

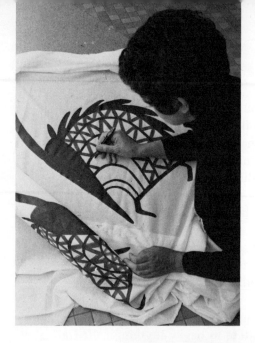

Working with felt-tip pen

Back view of caftan showing African symbols

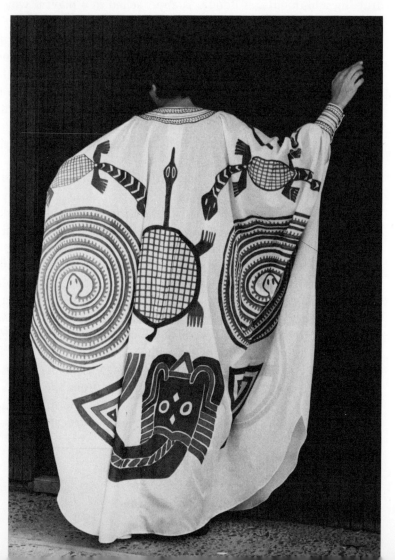

fish, a mask, and geometric motifs. The paper on which the motif had been drawn was placed over a piece of building board for support and the fabric placed over it. In using words with designs on garments, we have found it easier to work on the fabric after the material is cut to a pattern but before the seams are sewed.

The various designs carry a heavy freight of meanings in the African cultures from which they are borrowed. The coiled snake, for instance, supports the world. Should the world-snake become uneasy his nervous undulations cause earthquakes. This symbolism comes from the Fon people of Dahomey.

Sewing machine stitchery in black and brown cotton gives a typically African finish to the caftan. Pelon was used in the neck facing and the cuffs and paper was placed beneath the fabric to keep the machine stitching from puckering. This may be picked out after a garment is completed or it may be allowed to disintegrate gradually as the garment undergoes successive launderings or cleanings.

Young children seem always to have ideas about what to draw. Julia George spread a wide piece of muslin over a table and asked her kindergarten students to pick up felt-tip pens and draw whatever they liked on the cloth. The result was that the fabric was completely covered with bright designs, some of which were upside down because the children worked around the table. The enchanting result was made into a dress.

Dress made from drawings on muslin by kindergarten group

Various brands of flow pens with indelible or permanent ink were tried for washability and permanence. In general those which smelled the worst were the most durable. And it is best to try each pen on a sample of fabric before beginning a large project. The browns and blacks seemed more reliable than the bright colors and fabrics through which the ink could completely penetrate worked best. A cleaner line was obtained if the fabric was sprayed with Scotch Guard *before* using the ink. As someone pointed out, if the color does fade eventually, you just have the fun of doing it over again, so why worry?

A child's dress by Bici Linklater.
The designs and the words are in permanent
black ink on a pink fabric

A pillow by Beverly Nemetz in which the space
was marked off into smaller units

A hanging which is a direct descendant of a Bambara painted cloth from Kolonkani in Mali. Tanya Baker used some of the same shapes but assembled them in a rhythm of her own.

The work which developed in our workshop seemed most successful when the total space was first divided into smaller units of various sizes and then patterned. Often the addition of black lines gives sharpness and unity to a design.

The felt-tip pen and the doodle approach is a successful way to spark imagination and to encourage a spirit of play. Jean Hudson, who

Often the addition of black lines gives sharpness and unity to a design. Julia George made bright swirls of dye with a large brush across the surface of a muslin shirt. Some of the streaks of color suggested shapes so the doodling with a black pen began in that area.

teaches at a retirement community, asked her senior citizens to conjure up imaginary beings. Griffins, unicorns, and dragons were discussed and fantasy animals were encouraged. The group went along in good-natured fun but not very seriously. That, of course, was the problem. As J. R. R. Tolkien, author of the Hobbit stories, has pointed out, a fairy story is no good, and is not even a fairy story, if the magic is not taken seriously.

At the same time the older group was working at inventing imaginary beings, Jean worked with a fourth grade teacher. We expected the children to have more limber imaginations than the adults. The children were imaginative but in nearly all of their stories they expressed concern about what parents might say if they found out that the children were bringing to life unreal animals.

One story by a little girl told of finding a three-legged potato in the grocery store. She wanted the potato for a pet because "he smelled clean and it felt good when I put my hand on him." The potato had been rejected many times in the story because he was different from the other potatoes. He was very grateful to be loved and become a pet. The story ends when the child's mother sees the potato. She screams and demands that it be returned to the store at once.

Jean Hudson's experience with doodling in her own family was more heartening. Her son, Mike, who is thirteen years old, wrote his own story and illustrated it with felt-tip pens on glazed chintz. The story deals with the adventures of some armless creatures who had no individual names but were known by the number of spots on their backs. Mike's work is done in much the same imaginative, free-flowing style as Twins Seven Seven's.

Mike Hudson illustrating his own story

5

The Liberian
Rice Bag

Imagine a seamless cylindrical bag that will shape itself to whatever is placed inside it, a bag that will fold up into almost nothing when not in use, a bag that may be used over and over. This is the Liberian rice bag.

I first met this wonderful container when I went to Liberia to live in 1941. When I went on long treks to forest villages, raffia rice bags went with me containing not only rice, but also clothing, bedding, and gifts for chiefs along the way. I was completely captivated by my carrying bags. I found myself stroking their silky sides just for the pleasure of touching them. The natural dye colors became more beautiful as they aged.

Seamless fabrics have had a mystical appeal down through history. They symbolize wholeness and perfection. As I thought about this the idea grew in me that there could be great delight not only in using, but also in making these bags with my own hands.

I searched for a teacher. My first difficulty was in finding a man who would agree to teach this craft to a woman. Braiding rice bags is

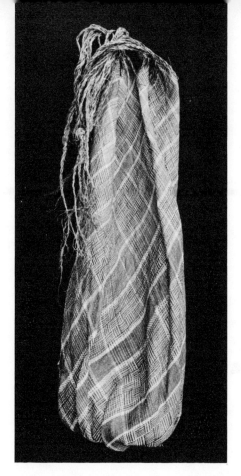

A Liberian rice bag, now known as a Peace bag. This one was collected in 1941.

work for men in the Liberian hinterland. All crafts are sacred and laden with hidden meanings in old tribal cultures. I had found a personal symbol of wholeness and health in this particular craft. Perhaps the man who finally decided to help me sensed how much emotion I felt toward it and it was this intuition that set up a kinship between us.

Although the man was willing to teach me, it was necessary for him to get the approval of the elders, both living and dead, before I, a woman and an outsider, could receive instruction. The living elders tossed cola nuts to divine the wishes of the deceased. Fortunately for me the four cola nuts which were tossed on a mat after suitable invocations fell face up. This indicated the approval of the watching dead.

My teacher could speak only a few words of English. He motioned to me to remove my shoes. I thought this was a symbolic gesture of humility toward the materials we would use. One may not begin any sacred craft if one's heart is numbed by pride. I then learned that the reason for being barefooted was a practical one. I was expected to maintain tension in the raffia by manipulating my toes.

It was soon apparent how little manipulative ability remains in feet that have been encased in shoes for years. My teacher announced sadly that although some sense might live in my head, my feet were "stupid past all." Finally, he made a circle of fibers, mounted the weaving strands on the circle, and tied it to a tree. He put his sandals on his own feet, I placed shoes on mine, and we were ready to begin.

When the Peace Corps came to Liberia, they were as enchanted with the raffia rice bags as I had been. Almost to a person, they began carrying them for purses. The rice bag was renamed the Peace Corps bag. Corps is difficult to say and the bag became the Peace bag. The new name is an added charm and gives another dimension to the symbolism of a humbly beautiful little article. It has been said that "remembrance is a form of meeting." When I see or use a rice bag, I am back in imagination with the Liberian people whom I knew and loved when I lived in the rain forest. Over the years on return trips to Liberia, I have had a number of teachers. The craft is no longer hemmed about with taboos; the dead no longer need to approve the student.

BASIC RICE BAG WEAVE

My attachment to the Liberian rice bag has led me and many others of our Crafts Fellowship to explore variations of the braid. Before one varies it, though, it is well to learn the plain cylindrical bag technique, the basic rice bag weave. This is very easy. As the work progresses, one small group of threads is interwoven with another. Each group is kept separate with a loose slip knot in order to avoid confusion. A good way to learn is to work over a roll of paper towels. Or, one may pin the work to a piece of building board and work around the board.

To begin, tie a cord around a towel roll or board and hang your braiding cords from this separate cord, called a holding cord.

How to Mount the Braiding Cords

Single ends of yarn may be tied to the holding cord with a simple overhand knot. Usually, instead of single ends, yarns are attached at midpoint of their length to the holding cord with a lark's head knot.

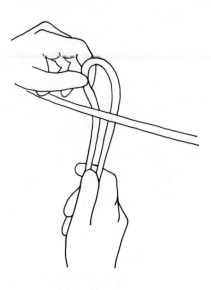

1. To make a lark's head knot, slip the loop of the middled yarn under the holding cord.

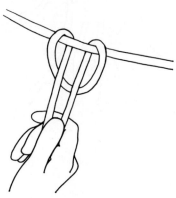

2. Bring the cut ends of the cord through the loop and pull down.

To make a small practice sample set up two units. For each unit cut 4 cords or yarns, 2 yards long. Mount the center points on the holding cord. This gives 8 loose ends hanging down from the holding cord in each unit.

In the drawings we have kept the units at a distance from one another. This is for the sake of clarity. In actual practice, they should touch.

With two units of 8 ends each hanging from the holding cords you can begin to weave.

Steps in Weaving a Single Unit of Rice Bag Weave

1. Find the two center cords. Cross the right-hand one over the one at the left of center.

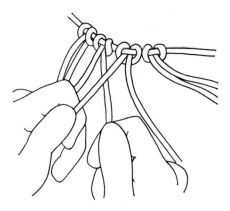

2. Pick up the first cord at the left of the crossed pair. Place it over the cord which came from the right half of the group. Now three cords are involved.

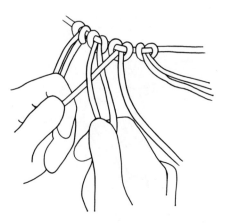

3. Pick up the first cord on the right of those which have been worked. Weave it under and over going to the left. Four cords have now been involved. Notice that the woven cords remain in the center area as one cord at a time is woven into the group.

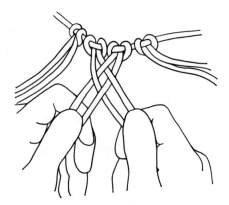

4. Continue in this way using a cord from the left and a cord from the right.

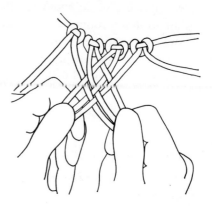

When all 8 cords have been incorporated, one at a time into the unit, a point has been formed. Four cords will protrude at an angle to the left and 4 to the right. This is one unit. (It might have been 10 cords instead of 8, or any even number.)

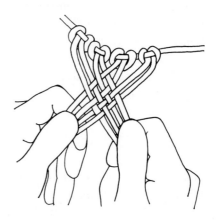

Weaving the Second Unit

Now weave the second group of 8 ends. Weave them in the same way, being certain that the first one on the right of center goes over the first one on the left of center. If one does not start each unit in the same way, the "unders and the overs" will not come out correctly when adjacent units are woven together. Set up enough units to encircle the towel roll or other object being used as a form. The Liberian craftsmen do not use any form for a guide but you will find the tension is easier to control if you do have something solid to pull against. It is important to have complete units. If 8 ends is the unit number and there does not seem to be room for the last group, try to push the units together to make room or else spread out the existing units so the form is completely covered without the last 8 ends.

After each beginning point is formed, tie the 4 ends that protrude from each side in a loose slip knot. The secret of good weaving is to keep the cords in their original grouping throughout the work.

What to Do About Tangled Yarns

A beginner may feel intimidated by long strands of yarn. The secret of untangling cords that do wind around one another is to pull on only one at a time. Imagine that you are a robin after a spring worm and be single-minded about getting the one cord you need at the moment. Don't trouble about the many cords except in a one-at-a-time manner. Some yarns are more likely to tangle than others. I find that a hand-spun yarn is usually the culprit when I do have a snarl but the added variety of texture in this yarn makes the extra trouble worthwhile.

Weaving Units Together

After the first set of points has been formed all around the cylinder you can join the points between any two units. Select a pair of points where you will begin. Pick up the top cord of the one on the right-hand side. Cross it over the top cord that issues from the left-hand unit. This is the first step of joining two units together.

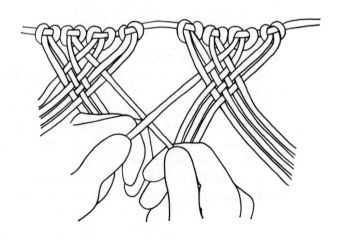

Continue weaving until all 4 cords from the right have been woven with 4 from the left and a diamond has been formed.

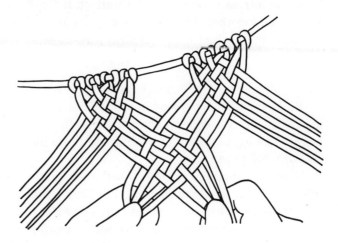

It is a good idea to tie each group in a loose slip knot to keep the units separate. Continue around the cylinder, weaving adjacent units together until a row of diamond shapes has been completed.

After each row there is an unwoven A shape between each group. The next row begins at the apex of any one of these A's. The cord near-

Weaving between the points

est the top of the A on the right is crossed over the one nearest the top
of the A at the left. One at a time, a cord from the right, then a cord
from the left, is woven into the unit until the 4 cords from each side
are woven together. This work continues around and around the cylinder until the desired length has been reached.

A BOLSTER IN RICE BAG WEAVE

Since the rice bag is woven as a cylinder, it is particularly appropri-
ate for covering a bolster. Ours rests on the hearth and is often pulled
out for use by anyone who would like to lie on the rug. It is shown in
color facing page 65.

A bolster should be made over the permanent form. When I started
mine, I did not have the foam rubber foundation that I purchased later
so I started work over a roll of paper towels. My tension would have
been much more even if I had waited to work over the foam.

Instead of starting with middled ends on a holding cord, I started
with single ends. Each was tied to a holding cord with an overhand
knot. Single ends were needed because the beginning ends were later
braided into points to cover the end of the bolster. I allowed 10 inches
for this above the holding cord but 12 inches would have made the ends
easier to form.

When mounting the cords, it was necessary to do a little arithmetic
to determine what number to place in a unit. I found I needed 144 ends
of heavy rug yarn. This gave me a choice of using 12 groups of 12 yarns
each or 18 groups of 8 each. I used the latter because I preferred handling smaller units.

The number of yarns needed always depends upon the size of the
yarn and the diameter of the cylinder. If 100 yarns are needed to encircle a cylinder of a certain size, 10 groups of 10 yarns each will work
out well. If 96 yarns are needed, 12 groups of 8 each is a good solution.

My bolster is 37 inches long. I cut each warp 78 inches to allow for
take-up and for forming the ends and the tassels. I wove the cylinder
around the towel roll for about 10 inches before the actual bolster arrived. The weaving was at that time slipped off the towel roll and onto
the foam rubber, which I had covered with a lining material.

The gathering braid was used to finish the points which I gathered
up to cover the ends of the cylinder. (Directions are given on page 66
for the gathering braid.) The overhand knots were taken out of the

beginning end of the bolster, after which groups of 8 cords were woven into points to cover that end of the cylinder.

If I were starting to weave another bolster, I would begin in the middle and weave first to one end, then to the other. This would give me shorter ends with which to work. I would tie the holding cord around the foam form at midpoint and mount each yarn with an overhand knot. After half the bolster had been woven, I would untie the knots, remove the holding cord, and weave the other half.

A TEXTURED PILLOW

We show two pillows in rice bag weave, made as cylinders. In one the emphasis is on texture. The yarns are close in color tones of red, oranges, and magenta with a small amount of burnt orange. There is great variety in the thickness of the yarns. In the other pillow, the yarns are all the same thickness but the variety comes from the changes of color. The colors were arranged to make a plaid design. The weaving technique is the same in both pillows.

The textured pillow is mine. Some of the yarn is rug yarn and some of it is hand-spun Mexican yarn as large as my little finger. When I

A textured pillow

hung the weaving yarns from the holding cord which was tied around an 18-inch piece of building board, I did not tie lark's head knots in the thick yarn. Instead I simply folded half the length of those yarns to the front and half to the back of the holding cord and anchored them to the holding cord with T-pins.

The yarns were cut 56 inches long. After being middled I had 28-inch lengths hanging from the holding cord. When the weaving was finished, I sewed the starting edges together with a length of red yarn. I might have finished the bottom in the same way but I decided to vary the usual pillow design by knotting the ends and allowing them to hang free.

I placed a covered pillow inside the weaving and tied the bottom yarns together, knotting a yarn from the front side with a yarn from the back all along the lower edge.

Making a Plaid Design in Liberian Rice Bag Weave

The secret of making a plaid in Liberian rice bag weave is to place like colors in groups. A sequence of color groups may be repeated around a cylinder.

Eight different colors in groups of 8 ends each were used to make the plaid shown. Each color was repeated in order twice, but to break the monotony of a regular repeat, 4 colors were used an extra time. This gave a total of 20 groups with 4 middled yarns (ends) in each, a total of 80 yarns. Each yarn was cut 54 inches long and was half of that, or 27 inches, after it was middled. The colors were yellow, yellow orange, red orange, red, dark red, magenta, purple, and gray purple.

An extra length of yarn was tied around the building board on which to mount the middled yarns with lark's head knots. The color units were set up in the color order mentioned above—8 ends of yellow followed by 8 ends of yellow orange, and so on, until all 8 colors had been used. Eight ends of yellow orange and 8 ends of orange were then set on to break the monotony before the entire sequence of 8 colors was again repeated. The colors seem to bloom and change as they cross one another in the progress of the weaving.

The weaving goes forward as in the basic Liberian rice bag weave. The first two around the boards forms points, and the rows that follow

Photograph by John Goldblatt, reprinted from *African Arts*, Vol. VI, No. 1

"Yemosa: Mother of Reproduction" by Twins *Seven Seven*

Liberian rice bag weave bolster by Esther Dendel

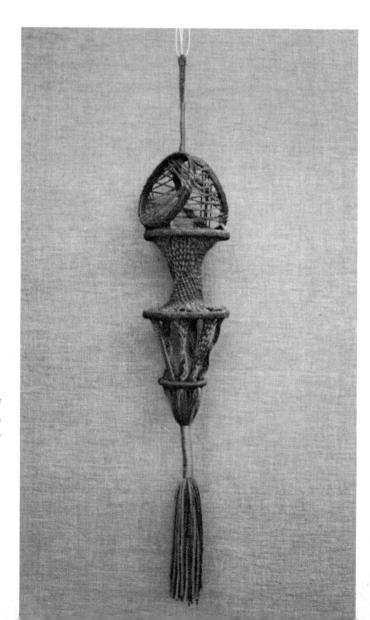

*Hanging sculpture of
Liberian rice bag weave
by Bici Linklater*

form diamond shapes. At the bottom of the pillow it is necessary to weave down to a straight line or a level edge. (Directions for weaving down to a straight or level edge are given on page 68.)

To fasten the pillow together at the bottom it was taken off the board and turned wrong side out. The front and back were tied together in sets of 4 yarns. Starting at one side, use 2 yarns from the front and 2 from the back. Tie one of the 4 tightly in an overhand knot around the other 3 and pull the knot up close to the edge of the weaving. After all the yarns are tied, they may be cut off a couple of inches from the knots.

A plaid pillow woven
by Cindy Hickok

Turn the pillow right side out and after it has been stuffed, sew the top opening shut with some yarn in a needle, taking small running stitches from front to back.

There are several ways to finish the ends of a rice bag weave. During the weaving process the working edge at any time is a series of points. The first decision one must make is whether to leave the edge in points or to braid to a level edge.

If it seems desirable to leave the points as they are formed in the braiding process, there are at least two ways to bring all of the ends along the edges of the points down to the tips.

Finishing Off the Ends by Overcasting

A simple way used in Liberia is to use the cord that is farthest from the point to whip over all the other cords, which are laid toward the tip of the point along the edge of the braiding. When all the cords from both sides of the point have been brought to the tip, they are braided together. The whipping or overcasting is done with a needle.

Finishing the End with a Gathering Braid

A second way of bringing all of the cords along each side of a unit down to the bottom where the cords from the two sides meet is called a gathering braid.

The gathering braid starts out like any pigtail except that each outside cord is taken *under* the center cord instead of over it as is usual in braiding a pigtail.

1. The first step consists of leading the topmost yarn under the second yarn from the top.

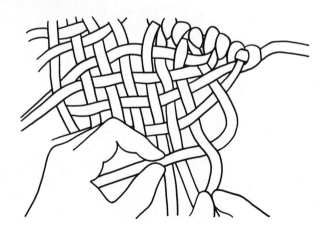

2. A complete cycle of ordinary pigtail braid is completed, using single strands. This is like any ordinary pigtail braid except that the outside strands are led under instead of over the central strand.

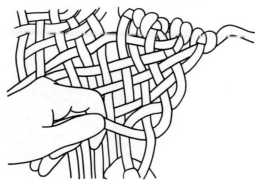

3. Begin in this step to gather up additional strands. The fourth cord down from the top is pulled under the pigtail and laid in beside the outside right-hand cord. As that cord comes inward under the center cord, the new added-in or "gathered-up" cord comes with it.

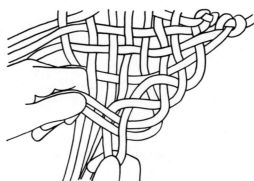

4. Continue adding a strand at a time to the outside curve as the braid progresses.

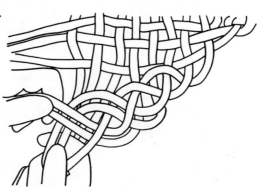

5. When all the strands along the side have been accumulated into the braid, it may project beyond the point of the weaving.

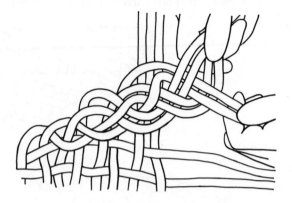

Since it is desirable to bring the yarns exactly to the woven point, the tension may be tightened as necessary. When the yarns from the other side have been brought to the point, they may all be wrapped or braided together.

Weaving Down to a Level Edge

My Liberian teacher did not think I was ready to leave his instruction when I had learned to finish off points in a neat manner with a gathering braid. He insisted I must learn how to weave down to a level edge. To do this, the first yarn from the right-hand side is woven through all of the left-hand yarns in the adjacent unit. However, the second cord coming from the right stops one yarn short of the point. The third yarn stops two yarns short of the point, and so on, until all are level. A level edge is desirable for zipper bags and in certain other instances so it is good to know how to make it. The old Liberian man who worked on this with me was enormously pleased because I, a woman, finally managed to make a straight line.

A TOTE BAG IN COTTON RUG YARN

Areas of wrapped yarns give pattern and distinction to a tote bag made by Frances Horsburgh. Cotton rug yarn makes a sturdy, washable bag. Two skeins each of rust and orange were used. The lining is a

Braiding the points down to a level edge.
Old Papa makes sure I do it correctly.

heavy brown cotton, which shows through the weaving in the wrapped areas.

The bag is 13 inches wide and 20 inches deep, including an 8-inch fringe at the bottom. The units were set up on the holding cord with a rust unit alternating with an orange unit all around the piece of building board over which the weaving was done. The handle is made in flat rice bag weave and is also lined to keep it from stretching and to make it strong.

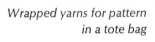

Wrapped yarns for pattern in a tote bag

In adding wrapping to a rice bag, it is better to use a separate yarn for the wrapping process rather than one of the weaving strands. Wrapping begins at any point and encloses all of the yarns in the unit on either side of a point. When the yarns emerge from the wrapping, they are regrouped, color by color.

HANGING SCULPTURE IN RICE BAG WEAVE

With four embroidery hoops and a smaller wooden ring, Bici Link-later made a delightful hanging sculpture which utilizes the cylindrical charm of the rice bag weave. Rug yarn in a medley of closely related orange-red colors was used.

The first step was to cover all the rings with yarn using a button-hole stitch or half hitch. Half hitching around a hoop is done with the ball of yarn in the right hand. The end of yarn issuing from the ball is held against the rim of the hoop with the fingers of the left hand. Bring the ball of yarn from outside the hoop to the inside, allowing a little slack to dangle between the left hand and the right. This makes a loop hanging down from the rim of the hoop on the outside of it. Now pass the ball of yarn from the inside of the hoop to the outside bringing it through this loop. Tighten the tension and repeat. What you are doing is a buttonhole stitch except that you work with a ball of yarn instead of a needle.

The ridge formed by this half hitching makes a place to anchor the weaving cords. Cut each weaving cord twice the desired length and middle it by threading one end in a needle and pulling it for half its length through the ridge made by hitching. The two ends then hang down ready to be woven.

The cylindrical weaving was pulled in to form a shape something like an hourglass. To attach the lower hoop each yarn was threaded in a needle and pulled through the ridge of half hitching on the lower loop. The photograph of a detail of the center section of the hanging shows the change of tension as the weaving approaches the hoop.

After the ends from the cylinder were brought through the ridge of yarn around the lower hoop, each unit was woven as a flat braid for a space of several inches. After each end was brought through the half hitching on the smallest hoop, all of the ends were gathered to-gether and wrapped, forming a tassel. The two hoops at the top were added last and loosely laced together with yarn.

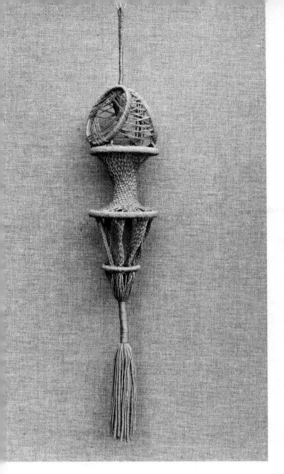

Hanging sculpture based on four embroidery hoops and a wooden ring. Detail shows changing tension.

Pattern in the Rice Bag Weave

Most of the Liberian rice bags are of natural raffia fiber combined with one dyed raffia fiber. Usually the colored strands are grouped in narrow bands which cross diagonally. One exceptionally fine bag which I collected in 1941 has a third color used in a patterned weave. Black and natural strands alternate to form squares and rectangles in which groups of stripes are at right angles to one another. The patterned areas are bordered by bands of red.

The key to the patterning is in the arrangement of the colors when the work is set up. Two black strands together at intervals and two white strands together at intervals vary the one-one alternation of black and white and cause an attractive pattern to emerge.

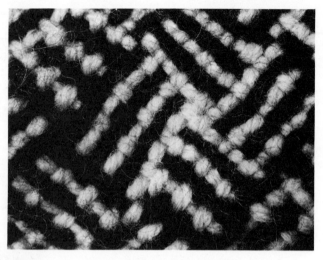

A purse in a black and white patterned weave

A detailed photograph showing the progress of the yarns

To test the theory, I braided a cylindrical purse. I set up the yarns in groups of 12 around a 6-inch metal hoop. The first unit was as follows: 2 black yarns, 1 white followed by 1 black yarn until 8 yarns had been added, then 2 white yarns to complete the set. To summarize the arrangement, if B stands for black and W stands for white, the yarns will be arranged: B, B, W, B, W, B, W, B, W, B, W, W.

The second unit is the mirror image of the first. It starts with 2 white yarns. Eight yarns follow, alternating black and white. Two black yarns complete the unit. The third unit began with black, as did the first.

In each set of 12 yarns, 6 braid to the right, and 6 to the left, as in any unit of plain rice bag weave. I braided each unit as soon as it was mounted on the hoop in order to keep the count more easily. A plain overhand knot secured each yarn.

The sets are compacted or spread out to finish with a complete unit that has the proper color ending. An even number of units is necessary. Using heavy rug wool, I needed 12 groups of 12 each to encircle the hoop. If I had used a finer yarn, more units would have been needed. Each strand was cut 1 yard long.

A roll of paper towels placed inside the bag while I worked on it helped to draw up each yarn to the proper tension. To strengthen the bottom of the bag, I used a round piece of untempered masonite (sometimes called hardboard) which was cut just slightly larger than the 6-inch metal hoop on which the cords were mounted. The masonite circle rests on the metal ring. None of this shows from the outside of the bag. The knots with which I mounted the yarns cover the metal hoop. Each strand was mounted on the ring 14 inches from the end. These 14 inches were used to weave the bottom and brought into a tassel at the center. To lead all of the yarns to the center, I used the gathering braid.

Weaving a Flat Area in Rice Bag Technique

It is quite possible to weave fabric using the rice bag technique even when the article is not a cylinder. The only new thing to be learned is how to turn the outthrust cords back at the edges. This can

*Flat weaving in
a loosely woven pillow top
by Eunice Ewing*

be used if you are making the front of a pillow rather than a cylindrical pillow cover. It is also used to weave a strap for a rice bag purse, or to make a belt or necklace.

If there are 8 cords in a unit, 4 of them will protrude at an angle at each side as soon as the beginning row of points has been made. The drawings show how to weave back the 4 on the right-hand side. The handling of the 4 on the left will be a mirror image of the steps taken on the right.

1. Pick up the topmost of the 4 end cords which thrust to the right and weave it back to the left by going under, over, under, the other 3.

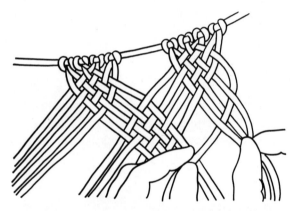

2. The cord next to the first one is woven back under and over, to the left. Two outthrust cords now remain to be taken back.

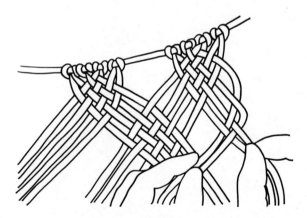

3. The third cord is woven back by going under the fourth.

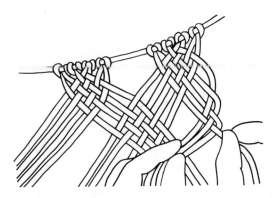

4. The fourth cord has no cord over which to cross. It is simply bent back to the left.

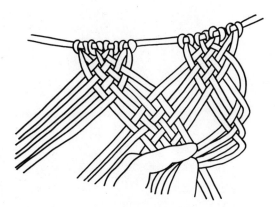

5. When all four cords in the end group point toward the left, they are ready to be woven with the adjacent group which points toward them, thus starting a new row.

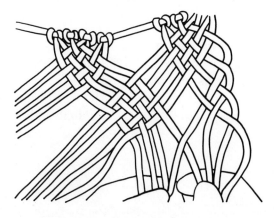

NECKLACES AND COLLARS IN RICE BAG WEAVE

Using her own variation of the rice bag weave, Annabel Bergstrom made a necklace using creamy crochet cotton. She middled 14 long cords, which gave her 28 ends in each group. Eight of these groups were needed to cover the metal neck ring with a clasp which she used as a foundation. Lacking a metal ring, one could mount the cords for a necklace or collar on a length of braided cord, leaving enough exposed cord to tie at the back.

Necklace of cream-colored crochet cotton with natural buff feathers

A collar, by nature of its shape, must gradually become larger the farther it extends over the shoulders. She did not add any cords to provide for this but, instead, loosened the tension of the work, which gave an attractive change of texture. Natural-colored buff feathers were wrapped into the points. The long ends of the cords were allowed to hang free.

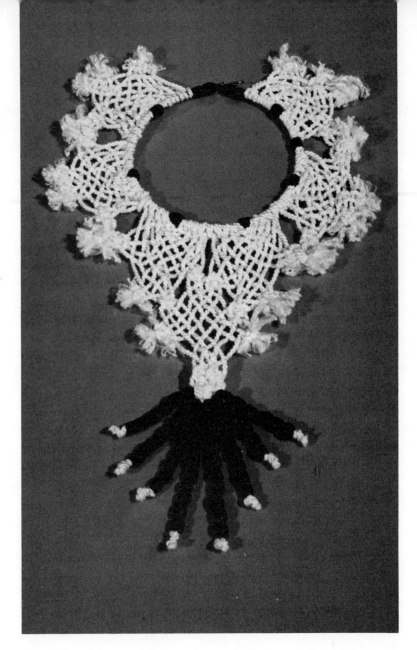

Black beads are used to weight this nylon necklace.

    Kay Gilreath used white nylon cord and black beads to braid a necklace. Four cords were middled to provide 8 ends in a group on either side of a black bead. After braiding a row of points all around the necklace, she joined 4 cords from each group with a square knot. The remaining cords were braided to a new point and tied except in the center front, where an additional row of braiding adds length to the necklace. The end cords were weighted by black beads strung on each cord. Eight cords were brought the full length of the necklace.

The only new technical problem encountered in the necklaces is how to handle the ends, since these pieces are not cylinders like the rice bag. It is the same problem as using the rice bag weave for a belt or the face of a pillow or any flat rectangle. It is easily solved by braiding the edge cords back to the left. This was described in five easy steps in the section on weaving a flat area.

6

African Looping

Looping is one of the simplest and most universal of all the ways there are to manipulate fibers. Looping may be loosely or tightly done, which varies the appearance greatly. In Africa looping is particularly suited for making costumes for ritual dances because when it is loosely done, it is flexible enough to accommodate body movement while at the same time it completely covers and hides the human being, including hands and feet, inside the costume. This is important in Africa because the dancing man does not just represent a spirit: he becomes and houses and is the spirit. The spirit-stuff of a god or a deceased ancestor flows in his veins. The rhythm of the drums is the force that drives it. The dance costume heightens the transformation.

I learned looping from the Mano women of Liberia. They use looped bags to carry fish from the river to their villages. Palm leaves are stripped from the trees and the fiber is spun as the looping progresses. The bottom of the bag is solidly worked for strength. The sides are worked over a stick which is later removed. This insures that the loops are even.

Bajokwe dance costume. Courtesy of the Brooklyn Museum

Sacred sculptures were often wrapped in looped fabric. This one is 20 inches high and from the N'Dema area of Rhodesia. Collection of William W. Brill

It is more than thirty years since my fish-carrying bag was looped but it is as strong and as beautiful now as when it was made. It is a natural golden brown color—a lovely earthy thing. I hang it on the wall when it is not in use. Perhaps the greatest treasure it holds is my nostalgia for the people and the place where I learned this craft.

My original looped bag. From Ganta, Liberia, collected in 1942

It is heartening to know that looping is still a vital craft in much of West Africa, one that is functional enough to live on even as industrialization sweeps across the continent. In Ghana in 1972 we found tote bags in the markets and on the streets everywhere. In the Ghanaian bags the handle is an integral part of the structure and the fiber is dyed in random patches to add color. Looped bags conform to the shape of whatever is placed inside them and they are enormously useful in any culture.

The Mano woman who taught me to do looping was insistent that all of the loops be evenly spaced and uniform. In using looping for decorative purposes, though, one works for variety in spacing and changes in texture. Perhaps before you consider some of the many uses for looping in our culture, you might make a small sampler to try out the technique and experiment with variety in texture. You will see that when each loop is pulled up tightly, the meshes disappear and the fabric appears solid.

Simple Looping Using a Needle

To begin, you need a needle with a large eye threaded with a yard or so of yarn or cord. You also need a shorter cord over which to begin the looping. This is the holding cord that holds the first row of loops. The holding cord is pinned down to a piece of cardboard or simply to a pillow, or to the garment one happens to be wearing. The looping cord is tied around the holding cord with any simple knot that will secure it.

To make the first loop, take the point of the needle behind the holding cord, then out toward you, bringing it over the beginning end.

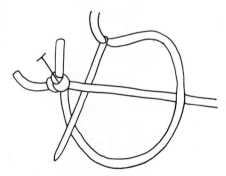

This simple act is repeated for the width of the sample. The looping advances from the left to the right. Tighten the loops as little or as much as you wish.

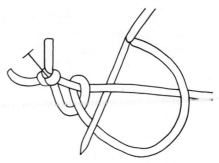

BEGINNING THE SECOND ROW

In the simplest looping each new row is begun by inserting the needle between the loops of the previous row. If the looping is started as a circle, the work continues in the same direction, left to right, row after row. To make the circle lie flat, two stitches are placed in a single space wherever necessary to expand the circumference.

However, if a flat surface instead of a tubular structure is desired, it is necessary to turn around and progress from right to left at the end of a row. The drawing illustrates how to make this turn, reversing direction.

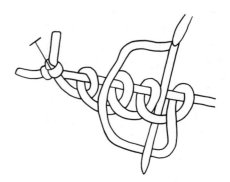

A number of rows of simple looping, one after the other, sets up a pleasing rhythm.

WHAT TO DO WITH ENDS

Before you have gone very far with looping you are sure to run out of thread and be faced with the problem of what to do with ends. When a Mano woman runs out she spins a new length onto the old by rolling the two together against the side of her thigh. We have tried that with yarn and with considerable variation in the success of the operation. Spinning on does take practice. Splicing by untwisting the ends of the fibers and rolling them together with a drop of fabric glue seems easier for most workers. A third method is to tie the ends of the old and the new cords together with an overhand knot and string a bead on them, making an accent out of a necessity. Sometimes, the ends can be hidden in loops previously made. Each looping suggests its own best answer to the problem of ends.

The looping we have been describing is a knotless netting. If each loop were fastened with a knot so it could not slide, it would be one of several kinds of knotted netting. A knot here and there gives stability to the work and is one more possible way to fasten an end of thread.

To make a knot, first form the loop in the usual way. Then, if one is working from left to right, insert the needle behind the loop just made and make another half hitch with the needle pointing to the right. Draw the thread down until it makes a tight knot.

If one is working from the right edge to the left, the needle points to the left when the knot is made.

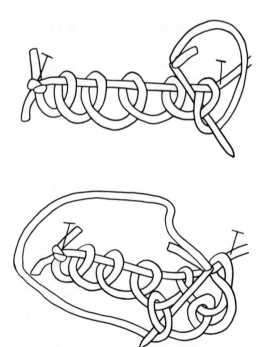

This kind of knot will secure the old end, which can later be snipped off. The new end may be embedded in this knot.

Looping and Twisting

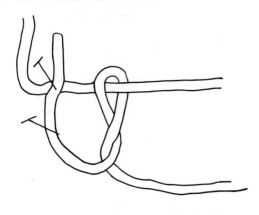

1. To give extra stability to a loop, the threaded end of the working string is sometimes twisted by wrapping around itself before progressing to the next loop. The working thread goes over, then under, the holding cord.

2. If the work is flat and it is necessary to turn back, working from right to left, the working end of the thread in the second row passes under, then over, the thread in the row above it.

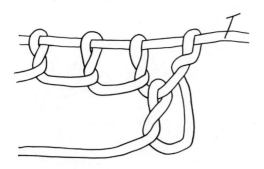

3. The twist is made and the working end passes to the left.

4. The work progresses by making the second row of loops around the thread between the loops in the row above it.

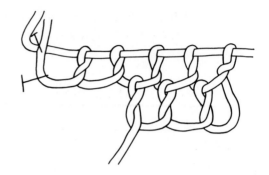

Working in this way keeps all of the twisting uniform in direction.

Looping into Loops

1. We have made loops between loops. We can also make loops which pass through the loops above them. This gives a firmer mesh than the other kinds and is often used in bags.

In making a tubular project it is not necessary to reverse directions. The work progresses continuously from left to right, around and around.

2. In turning back at the right edge, the working thread swings to the left.

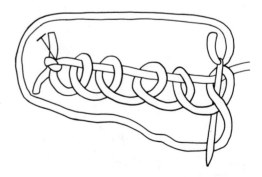

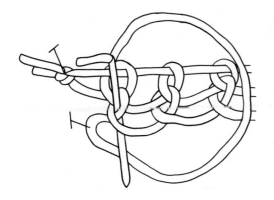

3. In turning back at the left edge, the working thread swings to the right.

Looping for the Knitted Look

If, on the second row of looping, one places the needle behind each loop above, instead of in the space between loops or into the loop itself, the work takes on a knitted look.

The appearance is so much like knitting that it is often mistaken for true knitting. To test it, cut a strand and pull on the broken end. True knitting will ravel back like a run in a stocking. Looping does not ravel back. In true knitting, the thread forming the loop does not cross over itself at the base. In looping it does cross. Knowing this simple test makes closely examining ancient and ethnic fabrics an interesting experience. A trip to a museum is much more exciting if you carry a magnifying glass. You will find looped fabrics labeled knitted even in good museums, and it is a quite understandable error.

A cylindrical tote bag of binder twine with added chain-stitch embroidery in black

Looping to Wear and Looping to Carry

Our Crafts Fellowship enjoys working with natural materials. Lacking a source of fresh palm leaves to strip and spin, Louella Ballerino decided to experiment with binder twine, which is used on farms to bundle grain in the fields. She made a cylindrical tote bag in the kind of looping that resembles knitting. The loops on the bottom of the bag were pulled up solid and make a strong support for whatever is placed inside the bag. The tubular sides of the bag were looped more loosely than the bottom. In starting up the sides, every third loop of the circular bottom was looped into. (The number of bottom loops skipped could vary with different projects.)

The black design of chain-stitch embroidery was added on top of the completed looping, with an eye to the intriguing proportion, as she is interested in the possibilities of dividing space. The black jute handles were sewn for some distance down into the inside of the bag for strength. An objection to binder twine as a material is that it is hard on the hands while one is working with it. Wearing gloves is one way to overcome this.

Julia George used ordinary jute string to make a sleeveless jacket and purse. She started with a string pinned to the shape of the neckline she wished and made the first row of looping over that. After three rows of looping, she worked the back and front sections separately. The back and front sections were again worked together beneath the holes for the arms. Toward the waistline, she tightened the tension and made smaller loops. The garment is loose enough to slip over the head and is drawn up snugly with jute string, which ties in a bow in front. The loops in the purse are smaller to prevent loose coins from falling out. This is a gay, lighthearted little ensemble made and worn in a playful mood.

Hand-spun yarn in natural light and dark tones was used for a collar by Helen Hennessey. Natural feathers were wound on the yarn ends.

A lighthearted jacket and purse

Dyed chicken neck bones incorporated in a collar

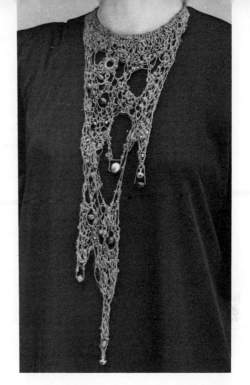

A collar of gold yarn with magenta beads gains variety of texture by the use of thick and thin yarn as well as the uneven spacing. The open areas set up a rhythm and are managed with great sensitivity. By Jonda Friel

If one works for unequal spacing, as she did, the empty areas, or negative shapes, seem to develop almost of themselves.

The bones of a chicken neck, bleached and then dyed a soft yellow color, were distributed throughout a large collar by Marvel Caliva. The cord she used for the looping was a commercial nylon twist that had dye incorporated into it. It had already been used for a tie-and-dye project and traces of the color remained as a changing tint throughout the collar. Ordinarily, this dye cord is thrown away after use.

WALL HANGINGS IN LOOPING

Because of its versatility, looping is enormously useful in decorative wall hangings of many kinds. Helen Hennessey used looping to

Collar in hand-spun natural yarns with feathers

make a fascinating hanging with thick and thin hand-spun yarns. Gossamer areas as wispy as spider webs contrast nicely with compact areas. This hanging was not preplanned. The weathered driftwood from which it hangs seems entirely in character with the natural colors of wool—white and tones of brown. The hanging seems almost to have grown from the wood.

Everything is grist for the mill when a craftsman looks at his environment. Alpha Salveson was on her way to a meeting of our fellowship when she saw that some unfortunate motorist had lost the glass from his taillight on the pavement. She immediately pulled to the side and salvaged the larger pieces of glass while traffic whizzed by her. In surroundings more serene than the middle of a busy street, the beauty of the broken bits of glass suggested a hanging in which light would play a leading part: light shining through the glass, and light shining through the interstices of whatever fiber might be used with the glass.

The first decision was how to anchor the bits of glass. Pocketlike nests made by looping seemed an ideal solution because it is possible

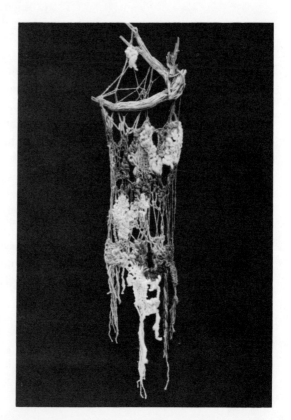

A looped wall hanging of hand-spun wool on driftwood

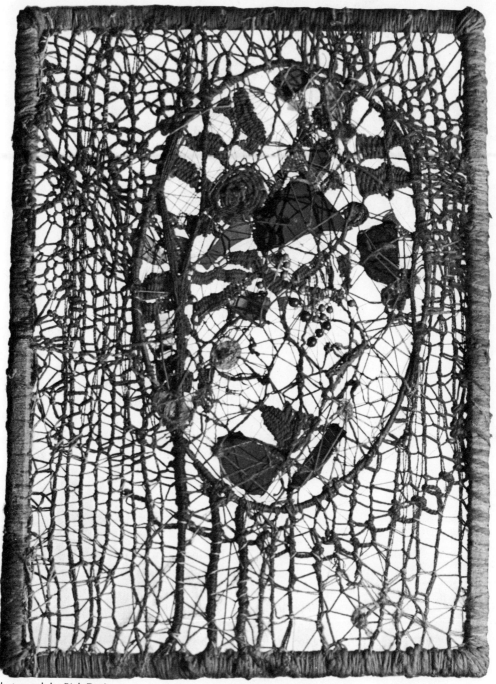

"Variations on a Color" with looped pockets for fragments of red glass.
Collection of Mr. and Mrs. Ed Mix

Mohair yarn on a wrapped hoop

to secure objects with rows of looping without completely covering them. It also seemed that if the color of the yarn matched the glass, the emphasis would be on light and space. The hanging is titled "Variations on a Color." It is designed to be hung where light shines through it. The inside oval was worked first within the confines of a bent-wire frame. It was then expanded by additional looping to fit into a slim rectangular frame.

Pieces of driftwood, pebbles, or any small treasures can be incorporated into hangings by making little pockets of looping to hold them.

Looping Within a Circle

Wooden or metal hoops are ideal frames into which to work looped areas. Sometimes the outside rim is covered by wrapping or half hitching around it. If the material of the hoop is interesting in itself, only a few hitchings, and those in an inconspicuous color, may be desirable. The hitching gives a place to anchor the looping.

Bici Linklater began her looping at the rim of her wrapped hoop. She used two layers of fine mohair yarn. When the circle is held against the light, the light works with both layers of color in an almost magical way. She found that she liked to finish off one length of thread with a knot, then start the new length of yarn back at the rim of the hoop, anchoring it in the half hitching. As a section of work approached the rim at some point opposite its beginning she found it was wise to pull it tight to prevent sagging in the center.

Others like to begin loopings at the outside edge, going all the way around the circular frame. Rosita Montgomery's hoop was a band from an old keg which had once been painted light blue. Some of the paint had weathered off, revealing the metal beneath. The yarns are of many textures, ranging from chenille to strands as thin as embroidery thread. The focal point is in yellow, shading down to golds, then into tobacco brown and dark blue. From the dark blue, the shading runs through many lighter blues back to gold at the outer rim. Unspun blue fleece tumbles out of the gold at the center of interest. Wisps of that blue are tucked into the looping in a scattering of places. The richness and variety of the colors and textures combine to make this a jewel in yarn.

Weathered, blue-painted band from an old keg was used as the base for a sculpture of pale blues, yellow, tobacco brown, and dark blue.

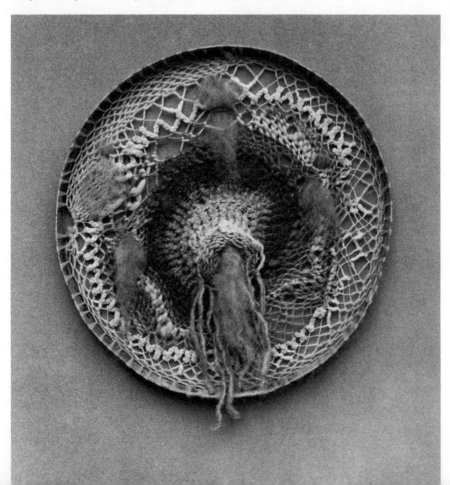

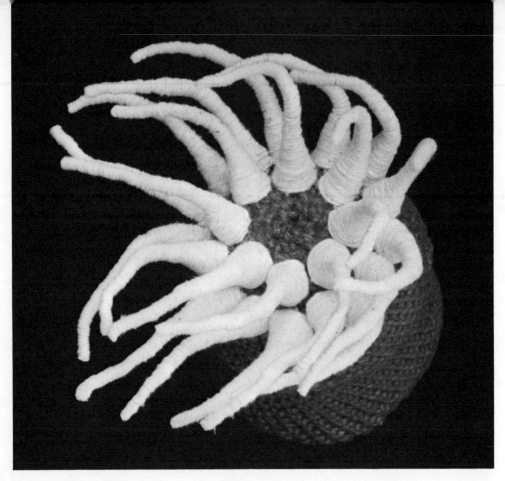

"Sea Anemone"

SCULPTURAL FORMS IN LOOPING

Three-dimensional netted pieces can run the gamut from a tiny play-thing to an environmental sculpture as big as a house. Francine Mos-kovitz experimented with a firm understructure made of loosely coiled rope beneath some of her looped sculptures. She wanted her work to be firm enough to be freestanding but soft enough to be responsive to pressures exerted during the course of the work. "Sea Anemone" is in red with white tentacles and is worked over a rope understructure. The spiral effect of the stitches of the looping as they pass over curved sur-faces is most attractive.

Another use of an understructure was made by Annabel Bergstrom. Her project was a mask and she worked over a wig stand. Beginning at

Wrapped circles
and looping
by Lois Isenberg

Looping sculpture on bent and wrapped
copper wire by Doris Hoover

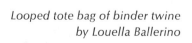

Looped tote bag of binder twine
by Louella Ballerino

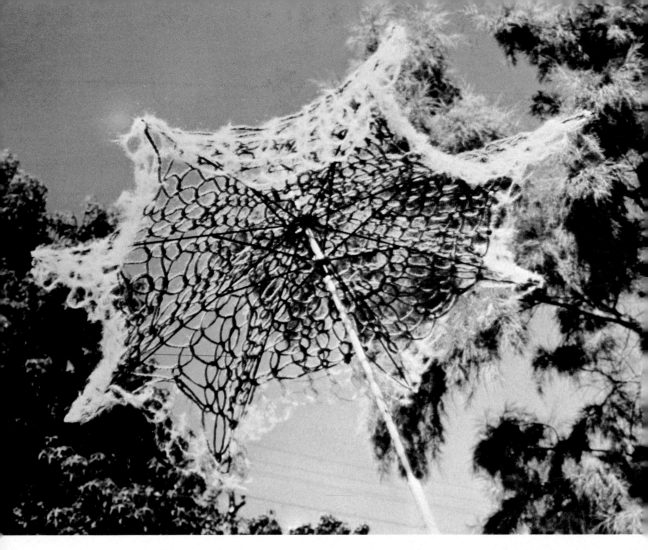

Hausa-inspired looped umbrella by Catherine Wallis

the center of the top of the head, she carried her looping around and around the form, leaving slits for eyes and mouth, adding loops to build the bulge of the nose. When the looping was finished, she added a raffialike fiber by middling the strands and tying them into the netting at the center of their lengths. A lark's head knot was used to attach this thick bristling of fibers. Fibers were also added beneath the mask in the manner of an African dance costume where the body as well as the face of the spirit-bearer inside the costume must be hidden.

Catherine Wallis's sculpture is draped over an understructure, also. She found a lovely old umbrella with a center stem of wood. The ribs of the frame were in good condition. She looped over the ribs to interpret a proverb from the Hausa people of northern Nigeria. Most of the Hausa live in arid country and consider that rain is greater wealth than gold. What better way to interpret their proverb, "The greatest wealth of any people is the rain that falls from the sky," than to make an umbrella that will let the wealth of the rain pass through.

This umbrella is hung as a decorative object in a high-ceilinged room, a constant reminder of the Hausa people.

An African-inspired mask looped on a wig stand

7
Palm Leaf Plaits
and Other Braids

In East Africa, particularly in Uganda, plaited palm leaves are used for mats, bags, market stalls, and even temporary shelters. There are many, many patterns and each pattern has a name. The same pattern may have different names in different communities. Patterns are passed down in families through generations and while one family may associate a design with one event or one proverb, another family will see a different significance in the same work.

The dry palm leaves are split into narrow ribbonlike strips with a pin or a sharp fingernail. The splitting stops short of the base of the leaf. The unsplit portion keeps the strips in order when the plaiting is begun. Usually, one dyed color is used with the natural straw color of the dried leaf. After the strips are plaited, they are sewn together by joining the edges.

The pattern is determined by the number of strands, the arrangement of color in the setup, and the number of strands crossed in the cycles of the plaiting. The outside strand is woven to the center, first from one side, then the other. When a strand reaches the center, it

Palm leaves split close to the base and the plaiting begun

crosses into the group on the opposite side and becomes the inside strand of that group. The possibilities for making patterns are enormous.

When palm leaves are used, they are sharply creased at the outside edges where they turn back into the plait. Most of us will be using other materials, yarn or seine cord or jute. These materials do not hold a sharp crease but this does not make any difference in the plaits shown in this chapter. It would make a difference if we happened to be doing some of the more elaborate plaits which use a plain palm leaf on top with a dyed one beneath it, which brings a different color value to the top when the material is turned at the edge and the crease is made.

"LIGHTS IN THE WINDOW AT NIGHT"

This 12-strand braid called "Lights in the Window at Night" I learned at Jinja on the shore of Lake Victoria. Two natural and 2 dyed pieces of palm leaf were split with a pin, each into 3 sections, giving a total of 12 strands.

When one is working with palm leaves the first step is starting the braid near the unsplit portion of the leaves. Since we will use other material, we will omit this beginning step and start by arranging the strands directly in their working order. A piece of cork board or building board is useful for pinning the strands in place. T-pins are strong enough to hold the cords. We have used rug yarn in two colors for the plaiting material. Allow once and a half the length desired in the finished work, in this case a belt.

With 12 strands, 6 dark and 6 light, cut the proper length, you are ready to start. The 6 light yarns are pinned side by side. Three dark strands are pinned next to them at the right edge and 3 at the left.

This is probably the simplest of the palm leaf plaits because the rhythm is over one and under one. Most of the plaits start out at the edge by going over two strands, but this one does not.

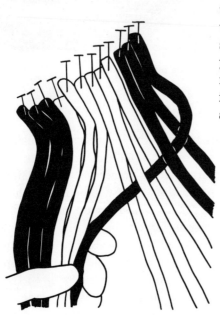

Step one consists of picking up the outside right-hand strand and weaving it over and under the other strands in the right-hand half of the yarns until the weaving strand reaches the center. It is then taken into the left-hand half of the yarns as shown in the drawing.

Two or more yarns may be used as a single strand, as Annabel Bergstrom did in her belt of rough spun natural yarn. At the right, this plait takes on quite a different aspect when braided in heavy Mexican yarn.

Step two consists of picking up the outside left-hand yarn and weaving it to the center, but being sure to go under the first yarn. When the weaving yarn reaches the center, it is taken into the right-hand group of yarns.

When the number of strands being used is an even number and one wishes to have an over one and under one rhythm, one side must begin as an over motion and the other side as an under motion. It does not really matter which is which as long as one is consistent.

"COWS IN A PEN," AN 18-STRAND PATTERNED PLAIT

This is a commonly seen braid in Uganda which is said to have been brought into the country from the Sudan. It has 12 light strands and 6 dark ones. Or, that relationship may be reversed, using 12 darks and 6 lights. We show it with 12 light yarns. These are pinned side by side on a board and flanked on each side with 3 darks.

The rhythm of "Cows in a Pen" (one of several names I heard for this pattern) is over two and under two. It begins with an over motion on both edges which produces an under three ridge in the center.

1. Starting at the right-hand edge with the outside dark cord, one weaves over two, under two, over two, under two. The weaving cord is then placed in the left-hand half of the yarns. This is step one.

2. The outside left-hand dark yarn is then woven over two, under two, over two, and under three. Before it crosses to the yarns in

the right-hand group, it will pass under the yarn which came from the right in step one.

These two steps are repeated without variation for the length of the plait.

Using a heavy rug yarn and plaiting rather loosely, the 18 strands of this braid yielded a belt 2 inches wide. Finer material would give a narrower belt. It is also possible to vary the width of this pattern by using more than 18 strands, but keeping the same color arrangement and the over two, under two, plaiting cycle. If one keeps a firm tension, it is possible to use a considerable number of strands.

"MAMA IS CHANGING HER MIND"

A very handsome plait is called "Mama Is Changing Her Mind." The alternate rows of dark and light zigzag so they seem to be coming forward and retreating, which probably accounts for the name. To make the setup, a dark cord is alternated with a light one as far as the center. A light cord is used on either side of the center. On the left of center, beginning at the outside edge, the cords are arranged dark, light, dark, light, etc. On the right of center, the same number of cords are arranged, beginning at the center, light, dark, light, dark, etc. Any even number one can handle may be used.

The plaiting cycle begins on the right side. The outside right cord

Detail of the plait "Mama Is Changing Her Mind"

moves toward the center, passing over two and under two, until it reaches the center, where it will go over only one. The plaiting cord then moves to the left side, where it becomes the inside member of the group.

The second step is the same as the first except that at the center there will be two cords (instead of one) over which to pass before the plaiting yarn joins the other side.

After one has experimented with the kind of plaiting done in Uganda, it is possible to look at a bag or a mat and figure out the setup and the plaiting rhythms that were used. In studying a bag collected by Elizabeth Douglas while she was living in Uganda, it seems obvious that the setup consists of 2 dark and 1 light strand and that the plaiting rhythm is over two and under one, except at the center, where there is an over three. If you begin plaiting in the right-hand half of the strands, the over three at the center will appear at the left of center. In the setup the two dark and one light grouping is reversed, bringing a light yarn on each side of center.

Detail of bag from Uganda showing ridges where plaits are joined. Collection of Mrs. Elizabeth Douglas

The photograph also shows two ridges which indicate where the plaits are joined. This is done by bringing a strand of raffia (threaded on a needle) behind the outside strand of one edge, then behind the outside strand of the opposite edge, and putting them together.

There is much more to be learned about the palm leaf plaits of Uganda. In the more complicated ones, the plaiting cycle does not repeat itself row after row. These plaits are very beautiful and are as intriguing as a Chinese puzzle.

Nigerian Chief's Robe Braid

Across the continent from Uganda in Nigeria, an 11-strand braid is made which is closely related to the palm leaf plaits of East Africa. It can be made in one color but usually 4 dark and 7 light strands are used. They are arranged with the 7 light strands in the center area and 2 dark strands on each outer edge. It forms a pattern and is used to

A bell-pull-like hanging with the "Nigerian Chief's Braid," in an experiment with different tensions. It is made in tones of gold and is mounted on a strip of brown silk. By Joan Coverdale

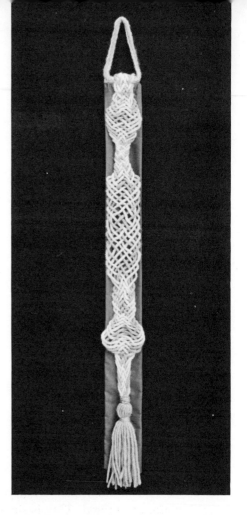

The "Nigerian Chief's Braid" was used as a decorative finish on this handwoven "Saddlebag for a Hearth." One of the delights of this saddlebag is the use of fine textured red yarn alongside a red rug yarn. By Helen Pope

decorate the robes of chiefs and elders, from which custom it takes its name, "Nigerian Chief's Robe Braid."

The braiding cycles are so similar to those of the Uganda braids that the braid can be learned in two simple steps:

1. Start with the outside dark strand on the left. Lead it over three and under two strands to the center, where it joins the group of strands in the right hand and becomes the inside member of that group.
2. Lift the outside dark strand at the right edge and lead it over three and under two to the center, where it joins the left-hand group of strands. It will cross under the dark strand which is newly arrived in the right group. Repeat these two simple steps for the length of the braid. Pull each strand completely through the other yarns after each move.

Jean Hudson made up a little verse to accompany the moves:

Over three, under two
Then to the other hand.
Over three, under two,
Makes a chiefly band.

Four-Strand Round Braid

The 4-strand round braid is found throughout Africa, and seems to be known in most of the world. There are many uses for this braid and there are several ways to make it. The method we show is easily mastered if you color the drawings in the book with felt-tip pens, using the colors we have used in the directions. These colors are white, black, yellow, and red, arranged in that order from left to right.

A hat in the form of a wig from the Museum of Modern Art's African show inspired a bright wig of many 4-strand braids. The original is from Zaire and was collected in 1951. It has a strap which goes under the chin decorated with two solid rows of pearl buttons. The wig may be worn as a gay party hat, or it may be used as a colorful, decorative textile when not being worn. The foundation is a crocheted cap. The braids are tied into this foundation. Rat-tail cord in bright red, orange, yellow, and purple was used.

*Bright-colored wig made
of the 4-strand round braid.
By Bici Linklater*

There are eight easy steps in making the braid. To begin, cut 4 yarns, 1 each of white, black, yellow, and red. Tie them in an overhand knot and pin to a surface against which you can pull to keep the strands taut.

1. Take white over black and yellow to the right. Let it hang down between the yellow and the red.

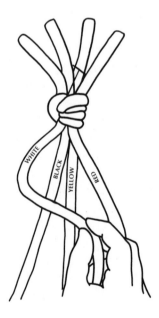

2. Cross yellow over black to the left. The order now is yellow, black, white, red.

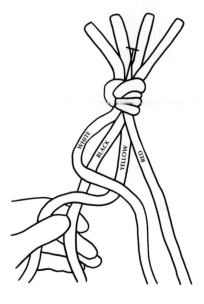

3. Take red over white and black to the left.

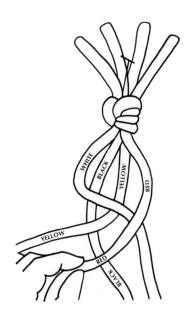

4. Cross black over white to the right. The order from the left is now yellow, red, white, black.

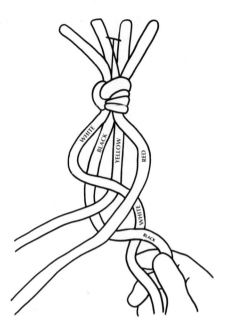

5. Take yellow over red and white to the right.

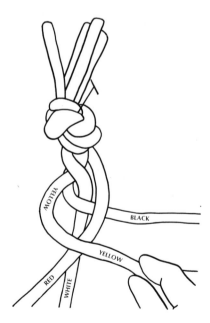

6. Cross white over red to the left. The order now is white, red, yellow, black.

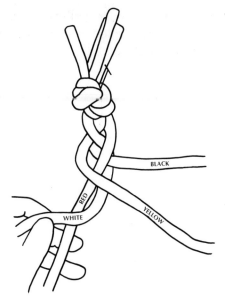

7. Take black over yellow and red to the left.

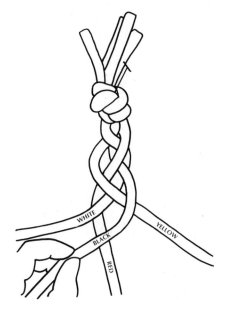

8. Cross red over yellow to the
   right. The order now is white,
   black, yellow, red.

Repeat from the beginning. After a few cycles of braiding, you
will no longer need to refer to the
directions but will have it in your
hand. As the braid grows in length,
the pattern of crossings becomes
apparent.

8

Dyes and Dye Methods

The dye women of Liberia say that God made every plant with beautiful color in it, but the knowledge of how to get the color out for man's use is a secret between God and the plants. Only certain deserving people, those with cool, clean hearts, may learn the secret. Indeed, the idea of coolness which represents composure and aloofness from the heat of petty quarrels is symbolized by the blue of indigo. The Yoruba of Nigeria have what the noted authority Robert Farris Thompson calls "An aesthetic of the cool," a concept which is also common in Liberia and Sierra Leone. Blue is the color of clean, deep water which suggests the fertility of moist earth, the wealth in streams and sea. Above the earth stretches the blue sky, which once was much closer to earth than it now is and which in legend is associated with the story of indigo.

While indigo is the very queen of dyes, other plants have yielded God's secrets and are in common use in Africa, particularly camwood and avocado. All vegetable dyes require a certain dedication to the task, but the reward in beautiful colors is well worth the effort. For

113

those who do not have space in which to work with bark, leaves, wood chips, weeds, and the like, there are good commercial substitutes.

Indigo can be grown in the southern United States, where it once was a commercial crop. Even in places where it freezes back in winter, it will often spring up from the roots and yield leaves for summer dyeing. It is a great satisfaction to grow one's own dye plants and have them handy for experimenting.

Many of the legends and stories about indigo which are told in Liberia mention the use of urine. The woman who taught me to dye spoke almost no English and I was never able to be certain whether she used urine or not, but the ammonia odor of the vat suggested that she did dissolve the indigo balls in stale urine rather than in water. However, indigo itself has a pungent odor and I may not have been able to distinguish between the two odors.

Indigo grows wild in Liberia. The leaves are beaten in a special mortar, not a food mortar, until they become a juicy pulp. Then the dye woman carefully molds the pulp into round balls about the size of a baseball which are set out in the sun to dry.

At the time I lived in Liberia, water was filtered through wood ashes to make "country salt" or leach lye, which was added to the dye pot. On more recent visits, the dye women were using caustic soda bought at a trading store instead of leachings from wood ash. However, in Nigeria the use of specially prepared wood ash is still carried on as in the old days.

When the dyer is ready to use the dye she will dissolve the dye balls in the liquid in the dye pot and add caustic soda. After stirring very gently in order not to introduce air, the pot is filled to the very rim with water and covered tightly with planks. It stands at least overnight. "It must rest for the work it is to do."

Caustic soda makes the indigo soluble so it will attach to the fibers of the cloth when it is introduced into the vat. It is difficult to imagine by what intuition the dye women of the tropical rain forests arrived at their formulas for successful dyeing unless one is willing to put aside disbelief in legends which say that "God allowed the plants to tell this to clean, cool women who love the things that grow and can talk with them."

Indigo balls are placed in the dye vessel in the sacred dye house.

Outstanding American authorities on indigo dyeing as well as other natural dyes are Fred and Willi Gerber of Ormond Beach, Florida. They are botanists by profession, but their enthusiasm for natural dyes has taken them thousands of miles to give workshops in which they share the information they have compiled over the years. In our home we have a bouquet of yarn on the wall, over 150 strands of exquisite color, each one a plant dye extracted by the Gerbers. We are sure the African dye women would say that these are people with cool hearts to whom the plants talk. There is a wonderful satisfaction in this kind of interest in plants and dyeing. More and more craftsmen are turning to the use of natural colors. The beautiful dyes obtained are only part of the reward; there is also the joy of hunting and collecting the materials in the out of doors and the challenge of becoming the kind of person with whom living things hold discourse.

In both Liberia and Sierra Leone, a beautiful rust color is obtained from avocado leaves, fruit, and seed. A fresh avocado seed may be carved and used for stamping designs on fabric. The color obtained from dye solutions varies greatly with the mordant or reagent used to fix the color. Copper gives the color which most closely approximates the rust tones which the African dyers achieve. Alum gives a lemon yellow, tin a gold yellow, chrome a brownish yellow, and iron a warm gray.

Dixie Mohan, who has done considerable work with avocado dye, gives this recipe: Plan on 2 pounds of avocado leaves for 1 pound of fiber. The more leaves, the deeper the color. Chop up the leaves and soak them all night in water. The next day, boil them up to extract the color. Strain out the leaves before introducing the fiber which has already been through the selected mordant.

If one does not have avocado trees, it may be more convenient to work for the warm rust color with iron rust and soda ash. This works like indigo in that the more dippings, the deeper the color, so it is practical for use with starch resist. Iron rust and indigo are a beautiful combination in two-color fabrics. Two vessels (enamel or plastic) are needed. Both iron of sulfate and soda ash may be bought at a drugstore. Iron of sulfate, or ferrous sulfate, is commonly called copperas. It is used as a mordant with many vegetable dyes.

To make the solutions, use 1 tablespoon of ferrous sulfate to a quart of water. Enough water should be used to cover the fabric easily. This

Julia George has used iron rust extensively in her batiks, which are both starch resist and wax resist. She sometimes combines rust with other, darker dyes. Her "Earth Mother" has rust in the lighter areas and potassium permanganate in the darker tones.

is placed in one vessel. In the second vessel, place a solution of 1 tablespoon of soda ash to a quart of water.

Dip the material to be dyed in the iron of sulfate solution and lift it out, allowing the excess liquid to run off the surface. Then dip the material into the soda ash solution and allow it to drain as before. If the material has starch resist design on it, allow it to dry before the next dipping. The depth of the color will range from a light cream to a deep reddish orange. It will be green when it is first dipped, but it turns to the final color when exposed to the air. Ten or twelve dippings give a rich, beautiful, deep color. The iron rust dye is quite fast. Some people with sensitive skin find that it is an irritant and that they must line clothing dyed in iron rust.

Permanganate of potash is a beautiful dye which can also be used as a bleach to discharge indigo and some other dyes. It is poisonous and must not be used around children. It is a beautiful purple solution, but yields a brown dye after the air gets to the fabric. It is most successful when used with other dyes, particularly iron rust.

Only 1 teaspoon per quart of water is needed. The fabric is slowly dipped in and out. Be sure all the crystals are dissolved before putting the fabric into the vat. If the fabric does not drain evenly the color will streak. If you wish to bleach this dye from the fabric, lemon juice may be used. The juice of lemon will also bleach any dye that splashes on the skin. As with all other dyes, rubber gloves should be worn when using it.

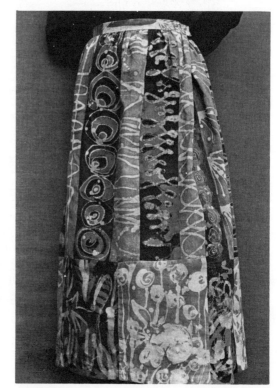

Lois Martin made a batik skirt with iron rust overdyed in some areas with potassium permanganate. She worked with narrow strips which were later pieced together. This is a good device to minimize the amounts of yardage to be handled at any one time of dyeing.

In tie-dyeing you can use any of the commercial dyes which are made fast by boiling. Even the fiber-reactive dyes designed for cold water work better at around 100 degrees, which is below the melting point of beeswax for batiking. We have experimented with nearly all the dyes on the market and recommend both Cushings and Putnams. Simply follow the directions on the package. The most common mistake in using these dyes is not using enough dye; then the colors are weak and seem washed-out. Salt is used with most commercial dyes to help with colorfastness. Test strips of fabric are recommended for all kinds of dye work. The fabric will appear darker while it is wet, so it needs to be dried before there is a true indication of the depth of color.

Inkodye is a simple, easy dye to use and it can be painted on the fabric. It is fast in color and may be used on untreated cotton, linen, rayon, and raw silk. The color develops with sunlight or by ironing.

Randy Hickok was so excited about the color-developing process of Inkodye he did not bother with starch or wax resist batik. Instead he painted his trousers freely in rainbow hues. His mother says they stand up under machine washing.

There seems almost an element of magic in the way a pudding-colored area gradually becomes a flaming orange or stunning red-violet, or even a dark-as-midnight black. The equipment can be cleaned up with water, which is another advantage.

After the fabric is painted with Inkodye, it may be exposed to direct sunlight. The colors are developed in about half an hour. A hot iron moved slowly over the fabric until the fuming ceases will also develop the color. Do not inhale the fumes, even though they are not toxic, only slightly disagreeable. After the color is developed, set it with an iron and wash and rinse to get rid of any residual chemicals.

Painting the color on the fabric is an economical way to use Inko-dye. It can also be extended with water for tie-dye or other uses where the fabric should be submerged.

The diversity of the Inkodye palette and the fact that the dyes can be applied as spontaneously as watercolors make them valuable assets for the craftsman working with dye.

Fiber-reactive dyes are a special class of dye made for use with cold water, which makes them suitable for wax batik. Since beeswax melts at about 120 degrees, hot-water dyes are not suitable, even though they may stain (rather than dye) a fabric in cold solutions. Salt and washing soda are used with fiber-reactive dyes. The salt should be un-iodized. The distinctive feature of fiber-reactive dyes is that the dye molecule actually bonds with the fiber. They are not suitable for starch batiks because it is necessary to soak the fabric in the dye for at least thirty minutes during which time starch will soften and dissolve. They are brilliant and durable when used on untreated cotton, linen, rayon, or silk. They do not dye synthetics or natural fibers treated to be wrinkle-resistant or drip-dry.

If dyes are not carefully used, they may be dangerous or damage health. A few simple rules need to be observed. Never use food containers for dye. Keep all dyes away from children. Wear rubber gloves when using dye and do not inhale fumes or powder.

The satisfactions and discoveries of working with dyes, especially natural dyes, are so rewarding that there is really no way to communicate the experience in words. One simply has to try it to know it. But as the Africans in their deep wisdom know, one has to deserve the reward of joy.

9

Adire Eleko ~ Starch Paste Resist

Patterning fabric by using some means to keep the dye away from parts of it is the basis of the resist techniques of tie-dye and batik. The fabric may resist the dye because it is knotted, tied, sewn, or patterned with wax or starch.

The Yoruba people of Nigeria are masters of the art of starch resist. Their starch comes from cassava tubers. Their traditional dye is natural indigo, a color to which they have a strong emotional attachment. The cities of Ibadan and Abeokuta are centers for the making of fine cloths but there are also compounds in Lagos, the federal capital, where Yoruba women work at their craft.

In the Yoruba language *adire* means "to take, to tie, and to dye" but it is used to designate all of their methods for reserving part of a fabric from the dye. Tied and stitched cloths are called *adire eleso*, while *adire eleko* refers to those that are patterned with starch paste. There are two common ways of applying starch paste. One is through the openings of a thin metal stencil. The second is more flexible and also takes much more time because each stroke of the design is painted

The adire *artist works in the midst of her children in her home compound.*

on the cloth, usually with a chicken feather dipped into a bowl of starch paste. *Adire* cloths are usually 2½ yards long and come in pairs which may be sewed together for a woman's wrapper, making an almost square cloth. Fortunately, they are made for the Nigerian people to wear, not for tourists, so the quality has improved rather than deteriorated with the years. My first encounter with these cloths was in 1941. I have been collecting new *adires* on each return trip to Nigeria since then and during the more than thirty years that I have been interested in the technique. I find not only more *adire* in the markets but better ones.

The *adire eleko* artist, who is called an *aladire,* sits in front of her cloth, usually white, which is stretched out on the ground of the compound. Patterning the cloth is a home industry and often a baby is tied to the worker's back while other children play about her. The cloth is sometimes divided by folding to make a kind of guide for the spatial divisions in the patterning, but the true eye and steady hand of the artist are the most important factors. The cassava starch paste is in a bowl in front of the artist. If it is an enamel bowl that has been chipped, the paste may be slightly tinted with rust, which makes it easier to see the starch lines. A chicken feather is dipped in the starch paste and enough adheres to it so that it works like a brush.

When one chicken feather wears out, the *aladire* simply gets to her feet, chases down a fowl, and pulls out a new brush. I once saw a goat walk slowly across an almost completed and intricately patterned cloth, stepping in the bowl of starch paste, almost as haughtily as if he knew what he was doing. Starch paste splattered in all directions. The artist calmly picked up the carved wooden comb beside her, dragged it through the splatters in a swirling motion, incorporating what might have been a disastrous accident into the design.

It is an absolutely engrossing sight to watch an expert *aladire* make hundreds of freehand, small circles with a feather. Her hands dance over the surface of the cloth with beauty and grace. There is one *adire* artist in Ibadan whose hands are so beautiful in motion that it is worth the trip just to watch her in action for a few breath-catching moments.

After the cloth is thoroughly dry, it is taken to the dyers. In Yoruba-land the dyers are women who store their indigo in pots. Each dyeing compound has many pots standing about so the women can move from one to another. The white cloth will be slightly puckered by the starch as it dries on the surface of the yardage.

Both fabric and starch must dry thoroughly between each of the many dippings the fabric goes through. If the fabric were dipped into the dye before the starch had dried, it would slide off in the dye vat.

Applying starch paste with a feather

The first dipping will color slightly all of the areas which are not covered with starch paste.

A really excellent *adire* may be dipped as many as thirteen times. I once tried to buy a cloth which was a light blue because it had been dipped only a few times. The dye women refused to sell it, saying that if I were to take it to my country, my people would say that Yoruba women do not know how to finish what they begin. The most favored dye job is so dark that it is called black. If it is overloaded with dye and the excess rubs off on the skin, it is considered a desirable cosmetic effect.

After its many dye baths, the material is wetted with water and the starch scraped off with a sliver of bamboo. The starch looks like blue mud as it piles up in great heaps. Often the cloth is given one last, quick dip in the dye after the starch is scraped off. This tones down the white areas and relates them to the dark blue tones.

It is a rare thing in the twentieth century to find a fabric on which so much expert care is lavished. We are lucky that the art of *adire eleko* is still vigorous and flourishing. Few of us can afford to collect African masks but anyone can collect African textiles. The most recent one in our collection came from Ibadan in 1973 and cost under eight dollars for the standard *adire* wrapper size—2 yards wide and 2½ yards long.*

Adire Eleko Designs

The designs on the feather-drawn cloths vary with each artist. Although there are traditional designs, two cloths are seldom identical. The stencil-patterned cloths vary as new stencils are cut, which is usually done by men.

Ibadan dun, meaning "Ibadan is a pleasant place," is one of the patterns traditional in Ibadan which varies in its details. It has a design of spoons interspersed with the pillars of an Ibadan building called Mapo Hall. Usually it has the stylized leaves of the cassava plant, which is the origin of the starch. It may also have the sun, the moon, birds, seeds, and geometric repeats.

The traditional designs have intriguing names. "Life is sweet," "All the birds are here," "Carefully done by hand," "Four friends who

*The Craft House adjacent to the National Museum in Lagos, Nigeria, is an excellent source for good Nigerian crafts, including carefully selected *adire.*

Ibadan dun,
or "Ibadan Is a Pleasant Place"
Collection of
Mr. and Mrs. Jo Dendel

should know what to do," and "Threepences are scattered around the house" are only a few. The name of the pattern is expected to start a pleasant train of thought in the mind of the beholder. "Life is sweet" refers to Olokun, the deity of the sea. Thoughts of the sea bring to mind the qualities of wetness, of blueness, of adventure, of delicious fish to be eaten, of coolness, of luck, of wealth from abroad. There is great richness in the lives of people who are trained from childhood to think in this manner.

One square of the Olokun *adire* I collected in 1941 has a curious crocodile with very small legs, a short body, a huge head with great teeth, and a long tail. Hovering above the crocodile in a solicitous manner is a bird whose body is almost as big as that of the reptile.

Detail of crocodile and bird adire

When I asked the *aladire* why she drew these creatures in this particular manner, she explained through an interpreter that a crocodile does not hurt one with its legs, so they can be small, small. The tail, on the other hand, is so strong it can cut a canoe in two with one swipe, so it must be drawn large. The teeth are so strong they can cut through the thick of a man's leg in one bite, therefore they are big. But after you are in the belly of a crocodile, you are past knowing where you are, so you don't need much room in there.

"But what about the bird?" I asked. I knew that some small birds fly through the open jaws of crocodiles basking on the sand in order to clean morsels from their teeth.

"The bird has to be big, big, because a crocodile feels bad if his mouth is dirty. The bird is big to the crocodile."

I rather suspect that there was something else behind these explanations which the woman did not know how to explain. I think she had a natural, inborn sense of design and for the use of space.

Stencil Designs in *Adire Eleko*

When King George V and Queen Mary celebrated their silver jubilee in 1935, special stencils were cut in Nigeria to mark the event with jubilee or coronation *adires*. The figures were surrounded by an oval frame of design motifs, which suggests that the stencils may have been inspired by framed photographs. Some of them have crossed swords above the royal couple and incorporate lettering, "George" on the left and "Queen Mary" on the right. As more and more cloths are printed from a stencil, the delicate portions holding all the sections together tend to wear and break down. As pieces of metal fall away, the areas

An adire *from an old stencil of King George V and Queen Mary's silver jubilee*

*An angel stencil
collected by Bici Linklater
in Lagos in 1973*

of combed starch increase. In some cloths made with very old stencils, the figures in the center of the medallion seem to be floating in a sea of blue swirls.

Mohammed's winged horse with a woman's head is a common motif in the jubilee *adires*. In a cloth we collected in 1964 in the big Lagos market, the body of the horse has become an almost unrecognizable blob with a tail and four legs but the woman's head with flying feathers is quite clear.

Recent designs may have the name of a new *oba*, or chief, and are made to celebrate his accession to power rather than having any reference to their British majesties. Other motifs include floral elements, space-filling dots, dates, and the ever-present Northern knot.

Old stencils are constantly being repaired. Ours, which came from Abeokuta, have many areas which are held together with metal clips. New ones are being continually made not only to have new designs but also because *adire* enthusiasts from all over the world enjoy collecting the stencils as well as the *adire* cloth. In some of the jubilee series, Adam and Eve have replaced George and Mary. In others, prayerful angels occupy the medallion area.

Yoruba tradition has it that long ago stencils were cut in leather,

Looped sculpture with yarns of many textures ranging from chenille to strands as thin as embroidery thread, by Rosita Montgomery

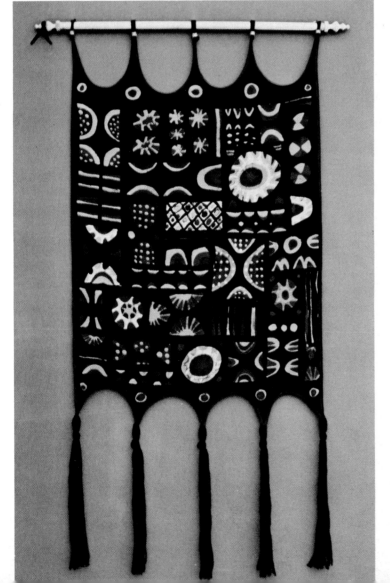

Batik on raw silk with African motifs by Josie Neal

*Pillow dolls inspired by
masked figures painted on cloth
from the Ivory Coast,
by Judy Whelan*

*Our first large fantasy doll, "The Old Belle,"
was a group effort.*

rather than in metal. We have not seen a leather stencil in Africa but one of our group made one and it works as well as metal.

ADIRE HANGINGS

Traditionally, *adire* cloth was made and used for clothing. Africans tend to wear their fabric art rather than hang it on a wall. Recently, two young African women have been producing *adire* cloths with a "right-way-up" and with focal points of interest, rather than all-over patterns. Both girls are the daughters of fathers who were part of the famous and vigorous Mbari group of artists from Oshogbo.

Senabu Oloyede, one of the two girls, is the young artist who made our 7-foot-long panel which she calls "Farming and Fishing." Senabu uses the traditional methods of the *aladire* but the designs are her own inventions and one of a kind. Like her father, the famous Asiru

A modern adire, *"Farming and Fishing," by the artist, Senabu Oloyede*

Wax batik shirt by Atanda of Oshogbo

"Spirits hear the drummer and come running."
Wax batik by Atanda of Oshogbo.
Collection of Laura De Lacy

Olatunde, who works in hammered aluminum, Senabu makes use of many leaves and trees as compositional devices. There is a sureness about her statements and great charm.

Since wax batiks are also being made in Oshogbo by young artists, it is useful to know that the starch batiks take the pattern only on the front side; the wrong side is quite uniformly blue. The young men of Oshogbo who work in batik seem to prefer wax as a resist. Since we first met him in 1970, we have followed with great interest the development of a young man named Atanda. Atanda's drummer seems to summon the spirits by the force of his own meditation rather than by his rather diffident drumming.

Atanda makes jumpers and shirts in batik as well as hangings. It is interesting to compare his crocodile from Laura De Lacy's collection with the earlier one in our 1941 Olokun *adire* shown on page 125.

Adire Techniques for American Craftsmen

There are a number of sources of inspiration in the *adire* cloths of Yorubaland for craftsmen of other cultures. One of the outstanding advantages of starch resist is that it avoids the potential hazard in the use of hot wax. This makes it a good process to use with small children or in schools provided the copper sulfate is omitted. Starch paste is less expensive than wax, which is another advantage. There are also certain limitations which are not really disadvantages, once they are understood.

The ingredients of the starch paste used in Nigeria have been given as cassava flour, water, and copper sulfate (to keep the starch fresh for a longer time). The flour and water are boiled until the mixture is the consistency of pap. It is then strained to remove any lumps. However, the *aladire* who have discussed the paste with us have all used another ingredient—alum. They refer to the copper sulfate which is blue as "country alum." The real alum which they buy in the markets comes in glossy chunks. We buy our alum at a drugstore where it comes as a powder. Alum is commonly used as a mordant or a reagent to fix the color in natural dyeing.

A young artist–craftsman, Lois Brooks, became excited about *adire* cloth while helping with the African collection at UCLA. She had always been interested in the arts of Africa and since the fabric arts are her first love, it was only natural that she did her research for a M.F.A. degree on *adire eleko*. She spent three years experimenting with the possibilities of starch batik and used natural indigo dye.

She makes a paste of pearl tapioca which she mixes with water in a blender. This paste is then added to a mixture of cassava starch, rice flour, gluten flour, and water together with $\frac{1}{2}$ teaspoon of alum and $\frac{1}{8}$ teaspoon of copper sulfate. The mixture is cooked in a double boiler.

Since we had some difficulty finding cassava starch and rice flour we experimented with a paste using only tapioca, cornstarch, and gluten flour. The following recipe was developed by Lois Martin, an artist who spent a summer researching variations of the paste resist.

Detail of starch resist on cotton velvet using natural indigo. Lois Brooks

1. Make tapioca paste: Combine ¾ cup pearl tapioca with 3 cups water and grind in blender until smooth. Let rest 24 hours. Blend again. Store in refrigerator and use as needed. (This is the same as Lois Brooks's formula.)
2. Dissolve in ½ cup cold water: 5 tablespoons cornstarch and 6 tablespoons gluten flour.
3. Combine in blender (until smooth): ½ cup tapioca paste dissolved mixture and enough water to bring total volume to 2 cups.
4. Cook, uncovered, in a double boiler over medium heat, stirring constantly for 5 minutes after mixture has thickened and cleared somewhat. It will be very thick, but will "string" off the spoon.
5. Place in working (not kitchen) container and add ½ teaspoon alum and ⅛ teaspoon copper sulfate. The copper sulfate may be omitted since it is only a preservative. *It is poisonous and should definitely be left out if children are to use the paste or be around*

it. Alum is astringent and unlikely to be ingested because it is bitter.

6. Mix thoroughly and stir occasionally while cooling.
7. Refrigerate, covered, when not in use—you will find it easier to work with if you warm it while it is in use.

Lois Martin found that she had the best results with her starch paste if she spread it on the fabric thickly with a tongue depressor and made her designs by scratching into the paste before it dried. Straight lines, curved lines, and dots all registered well. After the dyeing process, the starch may be peeled off dry or soaked and scraped off.

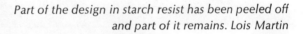

Part of the design in starch resist has been peeled off and part of it remains. Lois Martin

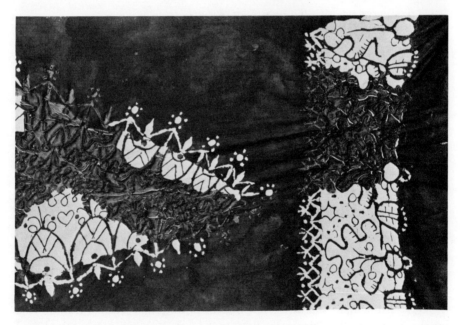

In addition to the paste one may make for the purpose, there are commercial pastes on the market. Inkodye packages a very satisfactory starch resist. It can be applied easily with a brush, just as though it were paint.

Detail of experiment using thick paste for design of straight lines, curves, and dots. Lois Martin

At first we were quite overwhelmed with the difficulties we encountered in a process which looked simple and easy when the Yorubas did it. We found that our most common mistake was to apply the dye before the starch as well as the fabric was thoroughly dry. Our next mistake was that we tried to dye in shallow utensils. In order to cover the fabric we had to squeeze it together. This placed starch areas against one another and the starch was pulled off in the spots that touched. We then went to deeper dyeing utensils or painted the dye on the surface instead of dipping the fabric. If one wants to dip the fabric in the dye, a plastic wastebasket is a good utensil (except for yardage in large amounts) because it has considerable depth in proportion to the width. Hot dye softens the starch more than cold-water dye so a cold dye is necessary.

Our enthusiasm for *adire* is boundless and threefold. First, it is a lovely example of African art which it is still possible to collect and own for the small amount of money invested. Second, the design inspiration found in *adires* seems endless and worthy of long study. Third, the technique is filled with challenge, and as far as we know has not been fully explored in our culture, except for the pioneering work in that direction by Lois Brooks.

10

Tie-and-Dye,
Sew-and-Dye

Tie-and-dye is thought by many students to be an older craft among the Yoruba people than the use of starch resist. Certainly, it is more widespread in Africa. Everywhere we have gone on the continent, from one coast to the other, we have seen tie-and-dye fabrics. It is a little difficult to know how many have been recently introduced by Peace Corps volunteers. We saw not only tie-dye everywhere but also Anne Maile's book on the subject being held by craftsmen who know no English but who can read the pictures.*

We would like to mention a few methods and techniques which seem to us particularly African. Mrs. Betty Okuboyejo, an expert dyer who lives and works in the Nigerian town of Ijebu-Ode, says that not only could an entire book be written about African tie-and-dye; a book could be written on nothing but the methods developed by the Yoruba people of Nigeria.

The use of raffia instead of thread for wrapping and sewing areas

*Tie-and-Dye As a Present Day Craft by Anne Maile. Published by Taplinger Publishing Company, New York, 1971.

A close-up of the raffia sewn pattern which is ready
for the dye. Dr. Joanne Eicher collection

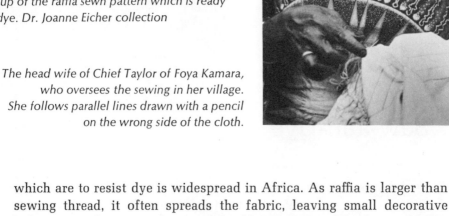

The head wife of Chief Taylor of Foya Kamara,
who oversees the sewing in her village.
She follows parallel lines drawn with a pencil
on the wrong side of the cloth.

which are to resist dye is widespread in Africa. As raffia is larger than
sewing thread, it often spreads the fabric, leaving small decorative
holes at regular intervals. Another characteristic of both tie-and-dye
and sew-and-dye in Africa is that it is nearly always done with two
layers of fabric instead of a single cloth. Possibly this comes from the
desire to have two matching lengths for draping the torso and the
shoulders.

In Liberia and Sierra Leone, the favored fabric is imported cotton
brocade, a match for the yardage which was commonly used for table-
cloths in the United States before place mats became as popular as they
are today. In the village of Foya Kamara, Liberia, near the boundary
of both Sierra Leone and Guinea, the head wife of the chief keeps forty
women busily sewing fabric ready for the dye baths.

The common African desire for a pattern of squares is achieved in
Liberia by sewing pleats together in straight rows at intervals across
the width of the cloth. After the dye process, the stitching is removed.
The fabric is then cut lengthwise in narrow strips and resewn so that

the areas which resisted the dye touch at the corners. If the pleated area which resisted the dye is 2 inches wide, the lengthwise strips are cut 2 inches wide, plus the width of a seam on each edge of the strip. The result is most attractive.

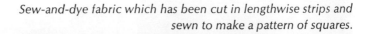

Sew-and-dye fabric which has been cut in lengthwise strips and sewn to make a pattern of squares.

Just why squares are favored in textile design up and down the west coast of Africa is not known. In Liberia, my efforts to find out led me to the conclusion that it is what might be called an "aesthetic of balance." The proverbs and sayings which were repeated in explanation referred to life situations. "The pot that is as wide as it is high does not fall over and spill the soup." Or, "The man who lies dead on the mat is the same long as he stood when he breathed." It was explained, concerning this last statement, that if an elder wishes to be honored after village. Proverb answers to "why" in Africa reveal rich and wonderful qualities of thought.

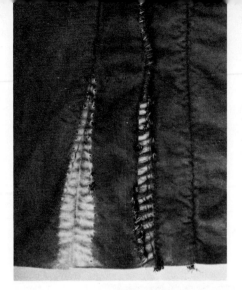

Cloth sewn with raffia in parallel rows and dyed. Two sewn rows are opened at the ends.

Not only the square but also the cross and the circle are widely used in West Africa. The sew-and-dye hanging with cross and circle design was collected by Mr. and Mrs. Ronald George in 1972 in Cameroon. This large cloth is particularly beautiful because it is done on hand-woven strip cloth made from hand-spun cotton. The age of this cloth is not known, but the cross may well have African pre-Christian meanings in which the vertical represents the path of the spirit from the moist earth, from which all life springs, to the sky above, where the spirits of the departed ascend. The horizontal arm of the cross, in this context, represents the people now living, the intersection of life now and life eternal.

The circle in much of Africa represents eternity—birth, life, death, rebirth. It may be drawn abstractly, simply a circle, or it may be pictured, as it often is in Dahomey, as a snake with its tail in its mouth. It is not enough for the African craftsman to make a pleasing or satisfying assemblage of lines and shapes. They must mean something. This is a knack we seem to have lost in our own culture.

A distinctive tie-and-dye is done in Liberia and in Sierra Leone, and perhaps in other West African countries, by combining wax batik with tie-dye. When we watched the process the source of the wax was discarded candle ends from a mission church. Wild bees are a possible source, but are fierce creatures to be avoided if possible. Carved wooden shapes were dipped in hot wax, then pressed on the fabric quickly before the wax cooled. The fabric was cotton brocade and the stamped designs reserved white areas.

The yardage was then clumped and loosely tied before being dyed

Sew-and-dye in cross and circle motif from Cameroon. Collection of Mr. and Mrs. Ronald George

Combined batik and tie-and-dye

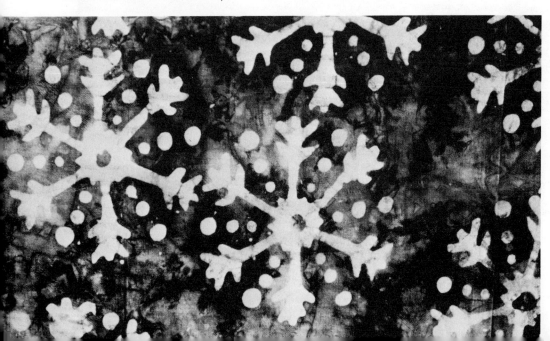

with avocado. After the yardage dried, it was reclumped and retied and dyed with indigo. After the completion of the dyeing, the wax was pressed out and the white star designs stood out among a field of rich rust and blue, beautifully mingled.

In their efforts to avoid encounters with wild bees, the Liberian dye women have collected wax crayon stubs from mission schools and use these for resist work. White crayons were especially prized until it was discovered that colored crayons yielded dye which adheres to fabric. Although it is not very permanent, melted wax crayons do give smashing colors.

One particularly African approach to tie-and-dye is to overdye a patterned fabric, often a striped design. When an old wrapper becomes faded, the overdye gives a new look. Overdye on patterned fabric often yields results of surprising richness and it opens up an entire new field for experimentation.

Tie-and-dye over a pattern of stripes from Dioula, Ivory Coast, collected in 1968 by Susan Vogel. Courtesy of the Field Museum of Natural History, Chicago

11

The Congenial Activity of Making Dolls

Perhaps no other single fact reveals so much about a culture, or about a person, as the way it or he chooses to play. Imagination, concentration, relatedness to other—all of these qualities are evidenced in play. Toys are the tools of play. Among toys, the doll reigns, a miniature queen.

Among the Turkana people of the Lake Rudolf area in the northern frontier district of Kenya, dolls given to little girls are dressed to portray the way the child will look as a young unmarried woman. Making the doll is a considerable undertaking. Wood must be packed in from Ethiopia, goatskin must be tanned, ostrich egg shells must be made into beads, brass wire must be found to decorate the arms. The father carves the doll, the mother dresses it.

Turkana women wear many strands of beads continuously, which stretches their necks from three to five inches. One of the delightful

Doll, collected by Lorilee Lance when she was living in the Lake Rudolph area of Kenya

Akuaba *doll from Ghana*

features of the doll we show is the use of a strip of broken zipper among the strings of beads encircling the doll's neck. The woman who dressed this doll saw the length of serrated metal as a form suitable for her purpose, not as a broken fastener. In other words, she was able to see abstractly and with imagination.

We cross the entire width of the African continent to study the next doll. This little wooden figure is called *Akuaba* and is common among the Akan people of Ghana. The doll from Ghana is not as literal as the Turkana doll. It is more of an ideogram of woman as mother-creator than an interpretation of human form. The moon was considered by the Akan people to be a visible symbol of the mother-goddess idea. We see the moon shape reproduced in the disc which forms the head of the doll. The arms are extended to form a cross at right angles to the short, cylindrical body. This suggests the dominion of the goddess over the earth and her protective function.

In former times barren women turned to the priests at the shrines to the mother-goddess. They were given an *Akuaba* to carry during the time they waited to have a child. For this custom, the dolls have taken on the common identity of fertility figures. Little girls are given the dolls to carry about in order that they may learn mothercraft from the creator goddess.

The first doll made by one of our group of craftsmen was inspired not by the African dolls we studied, but by flat designs of figures painted on hand-woven strip cloth in the Ivory Coast. These fascinating cloths were worn by hunters and by members of the secret Poro society in older times. Masked dancers, mythological animals, guinea fowl, and other creatures are drawn directly on the fabric with the edge of a dull knife dipped in dye. The Korhogo district is said to be the origin of these cloths although they are carried to markets as far away as Nigeria and Ghana. René Gardi reports that the traditional way of making these cloths uses two applications of natural dyes. The first is greenish yellow and made from boiled leaves. The second is from decayed swamp mud taken from between the roots of trees. Apparently an iron-bonding material in the mud causes the dye to combine with the coarse fibers of hand-loomed cotton to make a permanent color. Black ink is replacing the natural dye and machine-woven fabric has begun to replace the traditional cotton country cloth.

Masked figures painted on cloth

A pillow doll of Barbara Kincaid's has inside seams and is decorated
with machine stitchery, felt-tip pens, and hand embroidery.

A pillow doll by Judy Whelan

The masked figures painted on cloth intrigued Judy Whelan. They
inspired her to create a pillow doll in bright cotton which is decorated
with black lines made by sewing machine stitchery. Pillow dolls give a
distinct feeling of presence. They are good dolls precisely because they
do not bat their eyes or have simulated hair or speak. They do us the
honor of allowing us to vivify them with words and thoughts of our
own.

The idea of making imaginative pillow dolls inspired our summer
workshops and some large and exciting dolls came into existence. Fran
Silberman was in charge of producing our first large doll; the youngest
member of our group cooperated by agreeing to be the pattern. We
spliced newspapers together with masking tape and our model stretched
out, spread-eagle fashion, on the paper.

The two sides were not exact mirror images in the pattern, which
gave the figure immediate expression. We used old sheeting for the doll
and patterned it freely with Inkodye.

The flat head of the paper pattern did not form a three-dimensional
head, so we improvised simple features and sewed up the two halves
of the face and head with a sewing machine. The doll's hair was made
of narrow torn strips of fabric on which everyone in the workshop
painted a favorite word. She was provided with a loose blouse done in
starch batik and wears a string of African beads. "Float" and "dance"
were lettered on the doll's feet. She is stuffed with Dacron.

By this time the figure had so much personality it had to have a
name. "The Old Belle" seemed to suit her determinedly cheerful out-
look.

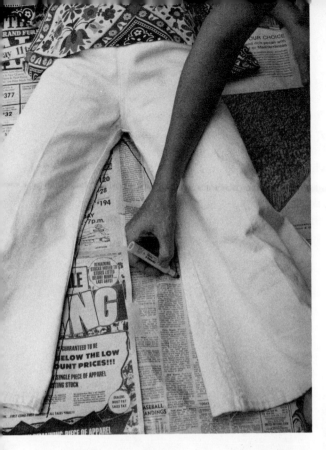

Our model forms a pattern.

Two sides of the face drawn for
cutting and sewing

"The Old Belle"

None of these dolls were made especially for children's toys but rather to provide adults with a way to experiment in an imaginative way. In Laura De Lacy's family, doll making became a project. Laura's own doll has visions of flowers which reflect in her eyes. Granddaughter Sarah, age six, made her own doll. It is a piglike creature which she painted and patterned in Inkodye. Stitching is a hand running stitch. Granddaughter Robin made her person doll from two pieces of print material. We can imagine no activity more delightful than doll making with one's own grandmother.

Barbara Kincaid experimented with making outside seams and using machine-sewn yarn as a finish. Her doll is textured with beads and with looping.

A smaller doll who emanates goodwill was made of old sheeting. Mary Ellis Arnett's doll has bead eyes and is decorated with felt-tip pens.

Piglike doll by Sarah Wallis, aged six

Laura De Lacy's flower-eyed doll

Robin Wallis's person doll

12

Ethnic Costume

The richness and variety of African dress is exciting not only to fashion designers but to anyone who wants his dress to express his personality. Flowing gowns, dashing headgear, patterned wrappers, elaborate embroidery, voluminous folds—all of these speak to us of the enjoyment of life, that elusive art in which African people seem so much at ease. A bony old man becomes a majestic elder as soon as he dons his robe. An ordinarily good-looking woman becomes queenly the moment a large turban wraps and emphasizes her head. The beautiful posture which is characteristic of African people enhances the garments they wear.

In older times in Liberia, the simple act of wrapping a length of cloth, a *lappa*, about the torso was a sacred and prayerful beginning to a new day. To each woman, the encircling of her body was symbolic of the circle of her family, her hearth, her ancestors, and her children, the continuity of life itself.

Various peoples have given different names to the clothing they wear, both their everyday garments and their clothing saved for festi-

Machine-embroidered caftan based on traditional design

vals and religious celebrations. The *danshiki,* for instance, was a small tunic when it received its name but now longer and wider garments are sometimes called by that name. Many of the variations in the robes men wear originated during their journeys to Mecca. It is an impressive sight to see an airport in West Africa jammed with white-robed pilgrims returning from their long journey and being welcomed home by joyful relatives, also dressed in their best.

A caftan is defined in the dictionary as a full-length tunic with long sleeves and a sash at the waist made to be worn under a short-sleeved outer garment. However, in common usage it often refers to any of the comfortable, wide garments that have a neck hole and are only partially seamed at the sides. Among the Hausa people of Nigeria, these robes are marvelously embroidered, either by hand or more recently by machine. Machine embroidery may at first thought seem to be a time-saving innovation but in actual practice it takes a surprising amount of both time and thread to really encrust a garment with embroidery.

Three Mexican rebozos which were as close in appearance to blue and white striped African country cloth as could be found were used by Mel Kernahan for her robe. Ideally, the fabric for this kind of robe should be wide enough to reach from wrist to wrist when the arms are outstretched, so the outside edges can be folded or thrown up on the shoulder if one wishes. There is no seam at the shoulder. The side seams are stitched at some distance in from the edges of the fabric and run from about the level of the knee to within a foot or so of the shoulder line. There is no seam to define sleeves.

The machine embroidery was done over paper as it is in Africa to prevent the material from puckering. The designs are traditional in Hausa robes. The long triangle is said to represent a sword. The arabesque is given different interpretations in different communities and is found as far afield as Liberia. One old man told me that it meant, "We are tied to all those whose blood runs in our veins." Most of the interpretations suggest kinship in one form or another. One man expressed this by saying, "The problems of my brother are my problems, also." This fairly simple design consumed thirteen spools of sewing thread.

A variation of the "kinship" or "interdependence" motif was used in hand embroidery on another robe. The original Liberian robe which inspired it has figurative as well as symbolic stitchery on it. The comb, the snake, the lizard, the leopard, and the human figure probably once had symbolic implications which are now lost to memory.

The original Liberian robe. Courtesy of the Philadelphia Civic Center Museum

An American version of the "kinship" robe done by hand embroidery and inspired by an early Liberian robe. By Patricia Wood

The only seams in the American version are one under each arm to establish the sleeve areas. The sides are open and hang loose. The embroidery is in fine wool yarn in two shades of gold, rust, and black.

The number and kinds of hats seen in Africa are endlessly inventive. Marian Sanders made a hat as much as possible like the Cameroon

Left: A copy of a Cameroon hat. The original was collected by Dr. Paul Gebauer in Ngambe in 1934. Below: Jonda Friel used the idea of mushroomlike protrusions in her hat, which was crocheted rather than looped.

Ibo appliquéd costume. Collected by Herbert M. Cole. Courtesy of the Field Museum of Natural History, Chicago

An evening shirt inspired by the Ibo costume

hat in the Museum of Modern Art show. Doing a project in the manner and style of the African original was an assignment in a course she took called Patterns of Art at the University of California at Irvine. The looping was pulled up snugly to give body to the work, the protrusions were stuffed, and the inside was carefully lined. The hat resembles the original so closely that there is no need to show the one which inspired the project.

The elaborate, appliquéd Ibo costume is made to be worn with a mask and, in contrast to the Hausa robes, is tight-fitting and complex. The Ibo appliqué inspired Cindy Hickok to make an evening shirt for herself. She worked over a black fabric which shows in the space between the various bright motifs. To achieve the effect she wanted, she worked with bias tape in red, yellow, and white. She wove these tapes with her fingers, then cut them to shape and bound the edges. The woven patches and lengths of rat-tail cord were sewn down with zigzag stitch on a sewing machine.

Ordinarily the pace of life in the towns that border the Sahara is leisurely and calm, but toward the last days of the religious celebration of Ramadan, the tempo of life changes. As this month of fasting and prayer draws to a close there is a movement of horsemen toward the nearest provincial city where celebrations called *sallas* are held. When the new moon is visible the emirs announce that the fast is over and great festivals will take place. There are wrestlers, snake charmers, sword swallowers, and drummers, but above all, there are feats of horsemanship. Each emir sits on a throne under an umbrella while wave after wave of mounted horsemen charge toward him. The riders reign in their steeds at the last possible moment and wheel into retreat. Their mounts turn away just in time for the dust to settle before the next wave of riders arrives.

The horses are beautiful animals and bedecked with bright blankets which are appliquéd and padded works of art. A rider often wears chain mail which is believed to have been left behind by lost Crusaders. The combination of chain mail and bright appliqué is dramatic and colorful gleaming through the dust raised by the flying hooves of splendid and spirited horses.

The jeweler Madeleine Marie LeProtti made her own elegant chain mail, link by link, and edged a padded appliqué collar which is quilted

Quilted collar
edged with chain mail

like the saddle blankets of the desert horsemen. Since the chains entirely encircle the collar, the weight of the metal is balanced and does not pull on the neck of the wearer. It is a dramatic and beautiful crafted accessory.

A DANCE SHIRT IN KNOTTED NETTING

A dance shirt from Liberia which was shown in the Museum of Modern Art's exhibition African Textiles and Decorative Arts was the inspiration for a knotted netting garment by Jean Hudson.

Not much is known with certainty about the raffia shirt. It has been suggested that it may have been used in ceremonies connected with the Poro, which is the secret and sacred tribal organization for men. Although I saw knotted netting being made for many uses during the time I lived in the hinterland of Liberia, I did not see any garment similar to this one. When women made knotted netting for other uses they always used raffia which they had spun. This shirt is made of unspun fiber. This suggests to me that it was made by a man because it is women who spin in Liberia.

Liberian dance shirt. Courtesy of the Milwaukee Public Museum

I think it likely that the shirt was made for use by members of the women's secret society, rather than for the men's secret society. When the girls come out of the sacred bush where they have been circumcised and rejoin the people of their village, they have what is called their "dancing time," during which no work is expected from them. They are encouraged to dress in their best and be carefree and lighthearted before they assume the hard work and responsibility which is the way of life for a woman in interior Liberia. It is the women who must plant and tend the crops because woman is the bearer of new life and increase. Field work is done in addition to bearing children, cooking food, and pleasing husbands.

George Schwab in *Tribes of the Liberian Hinterland* describes raffia shirts made by the brothers of girls who are in the sacred bush. He observed this among the Tie people. The shirts were made for the girls to wear when they emerged from the bush and began their dancing days. An interesting ceremony described by Dr. Schwab is the ceremonial burning of all the dancing shirts in one big fire when the dancing days end, as end they must. The woman who has had charge of the girls while they were in the sacred bush decides when to gather up the shirts. On the day of the fire, adult responsibilities begin.

Jean Hudson was intrigued with the Liberian dance shirt from the moment she saw it. She turned over in her mind ways in which she might adapt the idea for a dancing shirt of her own. When she enrolled in Patterns of Art part of the course was to try to understand the way of life and of art in another culture by making something in the manner in which the people of that culture would do it; to experience insofar as possible what an unknown maker of something had experienced. Making the dance shirt seemed the most exciting way to project herself into the life of a village in the rain forests of West Africa.

Lacking the natural raffia from which the original shirt was made, Jean decided to make yards and yards of 4-strand round braids (see page 107) to use for the knotted netting. In a round braid, the color in each of the component strands appears and disappears, reflecting light somewhat in the manner of a string of small glass beads. Beads, of course, figure largely in African costume. Braiding any of hundreds of various plaits is an African pastime generating serenity and contentment. I have seen Africans sit out a morning braiding vegetable fibers into long cords for which they had no immediate use. Joy in the doing was reward enough.

Had Jean wanted to do her shirt more quickly, she might have crocheted cords of good body and strength. However, doing something with dispatch and to get it over in a hurry is not the African way. Their way is to feel the material smoothing along through their fingers and palms without haste and in rhythmic growth. Another factor in Jean's decision to braid rather than crochet the cords was that a crocheted cord would not have yielded the beadlike flashes of color change that come from braiding.

Most of the material was shiny rat-tail cord, but some thick and thin yarn, some knitting yarn, and some chenille were used as foils for the shine of the rat-tail. The colors are bright scarlet red, blue-red, orange, purple, and gold. The cut pile edging at the bottom, at the neck, and at the ends of the sleeves was made of mohair yarn formed into pompoms.

Forty braids were used, each with 4 strands, making a total of 160 ends. Each was cut 114 inches long. This yielded finished braids 2 yards in length, as the take-up in this type of braiding is about one-third of the beginning length, with 6 inches for handling.

The first step after selecting the materials and cutting the strands was to make the 40 braids. Jean is deeply interested in the concept of *mana*. The rhythmic feeding through the fingers of pleasant material in flashing colors makes for a release of energy and for a return or renewal of energy: craftsman to material; material back to craftsman. Energy is circulating, spirit is renewed. The frantic world is far away.

After the braids were made, the knotting began. Jean started at the bottom of the garment, working around and around a piece of building board into which T-pins can be stuck. The board was cut 20 inches wide. A slab of plastic foam also works well as a form over which to knot a garment. Because the netting shapes itself to the body when it is being worn, no tapering is needed to insure a good fit.

An experienced knotter can work on one side of a board instead of around and around. After the garment had progressed some distance, Jean did place it on top of a board, working the back or lower layer and then placing the front or top layer of knots over the lower ones, pinning each diamond shape as it was formed.

The knot used to make the netting is one of the simplest of all possible knots, the overhand. The strand doing the tying goes around the cord being tied and the loose end is brought under and down through the circlet thus formed.

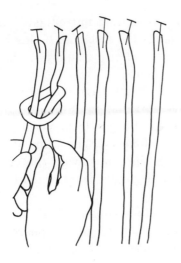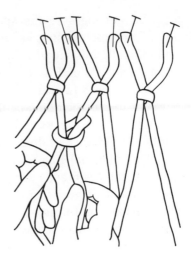

The plan of the netting is also simple. If you think of four cords numbered from left to right, 1, 2, 3, and 4, number 2 is tied over number 1, and number 4 is tied over number 3. In the next row, which may be spaced as desired, the cords are regrouped. Number 3 is tied around number 2. Number 1 (in a tubular garment) is grouped with the cord at its left, and number 4 is tied with the cord at its right. In the next row, the third, number 1 cord is back with 2, and number 3 is back with 4.

The dance shirt pinned to a board large enough to accommodate the sleeves.

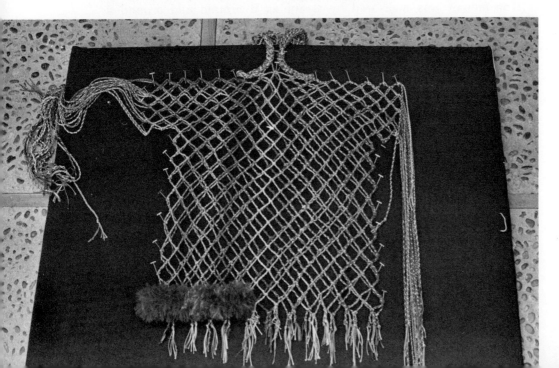

Jean did not measure the spacing in her netting but adjusted the placing of the knots, using her eyes to gauge the distance. If this had seemed difficult, a diamond shape of the desired size would have been cut from cardboard and used to space the knots.

The netting goes forward in a vertical direction from the bottom of the garment to the beginning of the sleeves. At that point the direction of the strands that are to form the sleeves changes from vertical to horizontal. The change of direction is made along a diagonal line of the netting. This diagonal line runs from under the arm toward the neck. At the neck, the braid ends are taken from the center front to the back to prevent the neck area from stretching.

Each sleeve was formed as a seamless tube just as the body of the garment was. Jean worked with both layers on top of the board. A beginner may find it easier to knot the sleeves by going around and around a roll of paper towels. The towel roll can be slipped down in the sleeve as it lengthens and pins can be stuck into the paper.

Mohair yarn in the same bright colors as the braids was used for the fluffy cut pile edging at the bottom of the shirt and around the neck and the ends of the sleeves. To achieve proper functioning as a dance costume it was essential to design a border which would not in any way restrain body movement or the movements of the braids themselves. Jean's solution was to use each two strands of the braid ends to tie a little bundle of cut mohair. Since there were four strands in each braid, there were eight ends at each junction of two braids.

The mohair was measured by wrapping it around and around a cardboard, 4 inches wide. The ends of the yarns were cut at both edges of the cardboard. Each little bundle of cut yarn was then laid between two adjacent strands of braid ends and tied with a square knot.

A drop of fabric glue was placed in the twists of the square knot for extra strength. The ends of the braid strands were then cut off. They were buried in the mohair when it was fluffed out into pompoms. There are four little mohair bundles tied at the base of each overhand knot at the edges of the garment where the border is used. Each little pompom can move separately from the others although the band appears to be continuous.

Knotted netting has many uses in addition to the shirt shown in this special project. You will enjoy making bags, hammocks, and collars as well as combining it with other fabric and fiber techniques.

The second half of the square knot ready to be pulled tightly against the first

The finished dance shirt

Background Reading

Adrosko, Rita J. "Dye Plants and Dyeing." *Plants and Gardens* (special printing), Vol. 20, No. 3. New York: Brooklyn Botanic Garden, 1964.

Barbour, Jane, and Simmons, Doig. *Adire Cloth in Nigeria.* Paperback. Ibadan, Nigeria: The Institute of African Studies of the University of Ibadan.

Beier, Ulli. *Contemporary Art in Africa.* New York: Praeger Publishers, 1968.

Gardi, René. *African Crafts and Craftsmen.* New York: Van Nostrand Reinhold Co., 1971.

Gerber, Fred and Willi. "Indigo." *Handweaver and Craftsman.* Fall 1968 issue.

Herskovits, Melville J. *Dahomey: An Ancient West African Kingdom.* 2 vols. Evanston, Ill.: Northwestern University Press, 1967.

Kent, Kate. *West African Cloth.* Paperback. Denver, Colo.: Denver Museum of Natural History.

Maile, Anne. *Tie-and-Dye as a Present-Day Craft.* New York: Taplinger Publishing Co., Inc., 1971.

Rattray, Robert S. *Religion and Art in Ashanti.* Oxford: Clarendon Press, 1927. New impression 1960.

Trowell, Margaret. *African Arts and Crafts.* New York: Longmans, Green & Co., 1937.